ADAM KINZINGER

Biography
Renegade vision in a divided country

Sean Eldridge

TABLE OF CONTENTS

CHAPTER 1
WHAT DO YOU STAND FOR?

Even as a member of the House committee investigating the deadly attack on the US Capitol on January 6, 2021, the litany of heinous occurrences was too long for me to keep track of. Worse, President Donald Trump roused his followers for weeks to buttress his claims of election fraud, despite aides telling him they were bogus. Knowing it was probably unlawful, his lawyers assisted in the creation of a failed operation to send to the Electoral College phoney pro-Trump electors who would insist on representing the genuine results of voting in critical states like Pennsylvania and Michigan. Then, summoned by Trump to Washington for a "wild" day, his supporters launched a brutal mediaeval assault on the Capitol. Trump watched the police struggle on TV for 187 minutes and refused to order the assailants to stop. He stood by as his loyalist marauders injured over a hundred police officers and stormed the Capitol, carrying Confederate flags and yelling, "Hang Mike Pence! Hang Mike Pence!"

America has never seen anything like January 6, which must be classified as a coup attempt. Trumpism, now a movement with tens of millions of supporters, is deeply un-American. It aims to destabilise our elections, impose press controls, severely restrict immigration, politicise the courts, and polarise the public. This is a fact that requires us to reassess our fundamental beliefs. Do we want a democratic system based on free and fair elections? Can we discuss our differences in politics, ethics, and faith in a courteous manner? Do we value our diversity? For generations, our ability in dealing with these difficulties has made us the envy of the world. Do we want to throw away what the Constitution has given us? What do we stand for as Americans?

I stand for the ideals I learned in my formative years, before Trump, and before conservatism and the GOP began their slide away from policies and toward power at any cost. For years, I tolerated this trend, believing that it would halt while I enjoyed the Republican Party's House majority. With Trump's first impeachment, I was on the verge of voting for the Articles of Impeachment, which would

3

have enabled a Senate trial. When he was impeached for the second time on January 6, I voted "Yea," along with nine Republican colleagues. A record number of senators from his own party voted to convict Trump, yet he won because of the rules. To convict an impeached official, a two-thirds vote is required. The 57-43 score indicated that my party was still in its own wilderness.

My vote for the House impeachment article made me a target among Republicans while also earning me plaudits from the Democrats and independents who make up our country's vast majority. It also landed me a spot on the investigation committee. As a member of the committee, I had access to a massive amount of documents, video evidence, and testimony. I also met the people who devised and carried out Trump's plan to overturn the election, as well as those who were involved in its aftermath. No one, however, was affected as directly—or even close to as directly—as the greatly outnumbered police officers. At 1:00 p.m., the officers began defending the Capitol as the attackers breached the poorly staffed barriers in front of the building. Faced with an outnumbered mob armed with two-by-fours and poisonous sprays and wearing helmets and body armour, the police retreated to positions inside the structure. More than a thousand attackers attacked them in waves, breaking through windows and doors. Hundreds gathered around a single door at times, pressing in a bizarre beat and chanting, "Heave-ho! Heave-ho!" It seemed like a child's imagination of a mediaeval fight at moments. In fact, they were not children, but rather older men and women, and they were not amusing themselves. They were determined to prevent Congress from certifying Joe Biden's election as President. Some of the cops who had defended the Capitol from the crowd on January 6 testified before our committee at its first public session about six months after the attack. I'd met each of them and heard how much they'd been through, so it wasn't abstract to me when Harry Dunn recounted the racist slurs flung at him and Aquilino Gonell condemned the "continuous and shocking attempt to ignore or try to destroy the truth of what truly happened." Michael Fanone described being pulled to the ground by a gang of assailants who threatened to kill him with his own gun. They did manage to seize his police Taser and shoot him, resulting in a heart attack. Knowing that the entire world had seen a video of him losing a fight

4

must have hurt Fanone, who appears to be a tough guy. He did not dwell on how he suffered during the hearing, instead focusing on the important events of the day and the aftermath. "I feel like I went to hell and back" to defend lawmakers. "But too many are now telling me that hell doesn't exist, or that hell wasn't actually that bad."

Nothing the police said made me think they were defeated, but their shoulders stooped and grief covered their faces at times, and it was evident their pain lasted. A lump formed in my throat as they spoke. They reminded me of troops who had become like family, connected by battle, and who I would always admire and sympathise with. "You guys may individually feel a little broken," I stated when I got a chance to speak. You all discuss the effects you have to deal with, as well as the influence of that day." At this point, I was overwhelmed, and my voice trembled slightly as I added, "But you guys won." "You hung on." "Democracies are not defined by our bad days," I responded, having recovered somewhat. How we recover from tough days defines us. How we accept responsibility for that." "Our mission is simple," I remarked, sweeping away the heated rhetoric surrounding our committee. Its purpose is to discover the truth and ensure responsibility."

After the policemen finished testifying, Fanone and I hugged. The weight he placed on my shoulder surprised me. Of course, I understood how the mob had yelled for his execution and how several members of Congress, whom he had tried to save, had now rejected the gravity of the attack in order to remain in Donald Trump's good graces. Their views were even more cowardly because they had witnessed the attack and saw the damage it had caused to people like Fanone, the institution that is Congress, and the country. I felt privileged to have him lean on me a little because the weight he carries—the sounds, images, smell of tear gas, and the fear that he was about to be killed by a political mob—is unfathomable. He will feel it long after the post-January 6 generations have reached adulthood and the memory of that day has faded. Those who do think about January 6 will most certainly focus on President Trump's evident crimes and the numerous efforts, including ours, to hold him accountable. After more than a year of committee work, during which members and staff interviewed over a thousand persons and received over 140 thousand documents, I understand that it can be difficult to recognize anyone other than Trump in this event. But then, in a split second, my mind recalls seeing those policemen testifying and hugging one of them, and that day stands out for the optimism it brought in a very dark moment.

After the hearing, I did what I always do after I'm done with my work for the week. I travelled to a private airstrip in Maryland where I store the single-engine plane I fly between Washington and Illinois. This small airport is the closest one that allows you to travel around the Washington area without being led by air traffic control all the way. You only need to announce the corridor you'll be utilising to exit the area—I'm not sure why, but the one I choose is dubbed the FLUKY Gate—and you're ready to go. In the densely populated areas, I keep low, below the altitude of the huge planes, and only climb after I'm far clear of them. When most people learn you have a plane, they assume it's something expensive or that you must be wealthy. It's pricey, but a middle-aged plane, like the basic Mooney Bravo I fly, was affordable when I was single and remains so now that I have a family. Furthermore, flying has been in my blood since I was a child, going up with my father, who flew, and when you consider the expense of commercial flights and the time needed in travelling that way, a little plane makes financial sense as well. Yes, a commercial flight will get you from Washington, DC to Chicago O'Hare in nearly an hour. But when you include airport hassles and costs on both ends, as well as the hour-long trip to my house in rural Illinois, there's no doubt that the Mooney is the better alternative. The flight also allows me to decompress. As I go across the Appalachian Mountains and see the farmlands of Ohio, I see a different America from the dominating political and economic centres on the coasts. This is the country that raised me, and while I don't cherish the resentments of those who believe they are disregarded as rubes from "flyover country," I am aware that they are spreading in a dangerous way. This is happening in part because too many individuals in Hollywood, the press, Wall Street, and Washington look down on folks from little towns across the country. But those of us who reside in these areas know ourselves to be nice, moral, bright, hardworking, and patriotic. We may not create much code, but we make and grow a large portion of what the country needs. Our youngsters make up the majority of our military's soldiers and sailors. This alone should ensure respect.

My home state of Illinois, where Abraham Lincoln began his public service, delivered America to the president who saved the country in its darkest hour. Without a doubt, he is the greatest president in American history. Every schoolchild in the state, I believe, takes a field trip to Springfield, where the Lincoln Museum, replete with records and relics, is located. The museum acquired Lincoln's stovepipe hat in 2007, along with his glasses and bloodstained gloves from the night he was murdered. The hat, which a private organisation purchased for millions of dollars and donated to the museum, turned out to be the wrong size. Although others defended the board member who purchased the hat with "nobody's perfect" arguments, she was fired. When my public grade school class visited the museum, Lincoln's hat wasn't there, but we didn't need to see it to feel inspired and even a little bit proud of where we came from. The man's attitude was consistent with the ideals we had learnt in our families, schools, and religions. Because of his faith, he stated, "my greatest concern is to be on God's side." His service was driven by his conviction that "you cannot avoid the responsibility of tomorrow by avoiding it today."

Our family enjoyed the kind of steady and secure life that everyone desires in our specific location, Bloomington, Illinois. My parents, Rus and Betty Jo Kinzinger, raised my brother and sister, Nathan and Chelise, to be the type of individuals Lincoln would have appreciated. My mother was a dedicated third-grade public school teacher who used all of her intelligence and imagination to help the increasingly varied community she served both learn in the moment and develop a lifelong love of learning. Every year, she taught an immigration section that culminated in a party in which the children dressed as their forefathers. They'd then act out an Atlantic journey in shady steerage, complete with a scuttling "rat" who was actually a well-tossed plush animal. My father worked in business, the state welfare department, the American Heart Association, and finally as the executive director of a faith-based group that provided a variety of services to the homeless. He put this private agency on a more stable financial foundation and then devised a novel way to increase revenue while increasing the sense of self-sufficiency in those who had previously come to the organisation for clothing. Instead of giving away everything, the agency created shops that looked like real retail stores and were manned by actual workers, not volunteers, who did everything possible to make these outlets appear and feel like regular retail stores. Customers paid little sums for the clothing they chose, and those who couldn't afford it might still obtain it. This method has helped numerous people feel more respectable over the years while also raising funds for more programs.

The stores were indicative of how my father solved challenges through a combination of knowledge, business acumen, and faith. Faith was an important element of our lives. The Bible was our direction and inspiration, and we went to church twice a week on average. We looked for churches led by pastors who focused on Christian principles and ideas that they held as ideals wherever we resided. What I remember from my childhood is a mosaic of play, school, and family that provided me with the kind of secure and happy life that epitomises the midwestern ideal. In the summers, a small gang of kids my age played sports, but also epic summer games of hide-and-seek that went until late at night. I missed a game whenever I was struck by a niggling health issue—proneness to bronchitis and asthma—that would keep me out of the game every now and then. I felt terribly unwell just after my first birthday when I contracted pneumonia, which might have killed me if I had not received competent care. This time, the therapy entailed spending several days inside a plastic bubble, which kept bacteria at bay. It's possible that my condition made me more sensitive to social demands. In comparison to today's archconservatives, I've always been more receptive to the idea that some people receive a rough deal and should be helped. No one in our subdivision worried about being safe in the area because we were. No one I knew was terrified of a neighbour's political or religious beliefs. I'm sure our family friends all had various opinions, but because politics and religion hadn't yet become yardsticks for judging others, I never knew anything about those aspects of their lives. I recall a pair of brothers named Steven and Craig whose house became a sort of mecca because they seemed to have all the toys and sports equipment in the world, and when home computers and computer games became popular, they were the first to have them. Gifts were typically exchanged on Christmas Eve, and birthdays were observed, albeit inexpensively. Christmas and Thanksgiving were spent with our extended family, of which there were many. Overall, we lived in a time and place where a substantial percentage of conservative Christians did not adopt a radical and rage-filled politics. Naturally, my parents' memories of me involve some oddities. They say I had a strong conscience from an early age, but I also had an independent streak, which meant I didn't simply accept what others said. For a few years, I used to cope with problems I didn't understand by walking around the brick boundary of our driveway, pondering as I went, until I thought I had resolved the issue in my mind. They dubbed it "walking the bricks," and while it was strange, they expected me to grow out of it, which I did. They also remember me as a child who, when presented with a difficult decision, sought their guidance but almost always chose my own route. I may have considered their point of view, but in general, I was more autonomous than dependent, and I did so because they had raised me to think for myself. Maybe those walks helped me develop this ability to think for myself, and their affection made me feel safe acting solely on my own conclusions. I ceased brick-walking by primary school and didn't confront too many difficult mysteries until adolescence, when I began to question some of the basic assumptions of the faith I had been taught at our church. The church, which adhered to the Independent Fundamental Baptist (IFB) tradition, mandated strict adherence to its principles and practices. Many of my peers become trembling zombies as a result of the pressure. I understood their point of view because I knew that most of their families adhered to a rule that linked their house, school, and church. As a result, any offence committed anywhere would be dealt with discipline administered by at least three adults. It was very simple to commit an IFB sin because so much of what others consider normal living is, in their opinion, an offence against the Lord. To illustrate how they compare to other churches, use a scale of 1 to 10, with the liberal Episcopalians, who have gay clergy, receiving a 1. Jehovah's Witnesses are at the other end of the spectrum, about 11 or 12. They are so removed from mainstream society that they will not vote or serve in the military. IFBs might get an eight on this scale. They refer to their congregations as "called out assemblies," a phrase emphasising the communal side of faith. Although each church is unique, IFBs generally hold the same high standards. They were and still are one of the few "no smoking, no drinking, no dancing" churches in the area. Other "no's" include listening to secular music, seeing most secular movies, and following daily dress restrictions. IFB wives are not allowed to work and must constantly be subservient to their husbands. Sex is only permitted in heterosexual couples. Everyone else should adhere to extremely conservative sexual norms. Every adult in the church community is to obey the children. Obedience to authoritative authorities, particularly pastors, whom many people think are anointed by God, is essential. Individual churches may enact tighter rules, but I've never heard of one doing so. And all of the rules are backed up by the fear of an eternity in hell. No surprise my church pals were frightened to do or say anything even somewhat subversive.

Fortunately, my parents did not accept all of the IFB rules as gospel. Their Christian faith was important to how they viewed life. They were and continue to be strongly opposed to abortion, and when faced with a dilemma, they may consider what Jesus would do in a similar situation. They never said that members of other churches were less Christian or that pastors were incapable of being simply incorrect. Did they agree that my mother should not work or that children should simply accept anything an adult says? No. They did not, however, join the IFB church in Bloomington because they agreed with everything preached there. They joined because they were looking for a church that would support their faith and make them feel welcome and comfortable. These things were discovered in a strong, cohesive society where individuals appeared to genuinely care about one another. The most strong benefit of IFB life is the community. It develops from the regular encounters of members who spend a lot of time with one another both within and outside the church. Many friendships are formed as a result of this shared isolation, which is aided by spiritual inspiration. If you are experiencing a crisis, such as a family death, or a wonderful event, such as the birth of a child, the church will be there for you, both spiritually and physically. And most churchgoers eventually choose to live by rules that relieve them of the weight of decision-making. Few people leave such religions unless they want to join an even stricter movement where they can feel even more superior. In the short run, the stricter the church, the more resilient it is. On the negative side of IFB cohesiveness, there is a lack of critical or creative thinking, as well as a tendency for people to see those who disagree and can't be convinced as wicked. Our family's tolerant attitude toward IFB rules inevitably resulted in "incidents." In one instance, I joined up for a midsummer bus trip to the massive Six Flags Great America amusement park north of Chicago, which boasted one of the world's tallest and fastest roller coasters. When I got ready to leave, the weather was 95 degrees, so I wore shorts. As I waited to catch a bus in the church parking lot, I saw that all the other lads were wearing long pants and all the girls were covered up so no one would lust after their knees. How did the young leader handle the situation? He directed the driver to take us to my residence, where I was directed to change. This did not sit well with my mother and father, but I still had a good time at Six Flags. And I overheard some of the attendees asking one another, "Are those kids Amish?"

Another famous "scandal" occurred when the church youth organisation, Singspiration, got onto a bus to drive to people's homes and sing Christian songs, as the only music we were allowed to sing was Christian music from specific accepted musicians. During this particular outing, I used the milquetoast phrase "Son of a biscuit!" which a younger child found quite amusing. When he started saying it loudly, a teacher who also happened to be his mother got on the bus, smacked him, and shouted, "Jesus knows what you're saying!"

Children reared in our church community face scrutiny, religious terror, and fast punishment, and they often adjust by disguising their genuine sentiments and being secretive about their activities. The stress of this could explain why the church schoolkids in my group were more prone to develop mental health or drug problems, as they were always watched over by the church. Adults who are under similar, if not more, pressure become liars and hypocrites, posing as sinless while engaging in affairs or indulging in the occasional beer. This is why, while speaking up in a prayer meeting or Bible study, folks will merely say something bland like, "I'm struggling," as they seek help. They are scared that if they admit to breaking a rule, the Jesus ambulance would arrive and transport them to the pastor for torturous "counselling."

The regulations and pressure to conform were designed to safeguard the church and its community from wicked outside influences, in addition to individual souls. For generations, a few verses in the Bible—one of which was "Be ye not unequally yoked together with unbelievers"—had prompted Baptists to forsake entertainment, the press, politics, much of higher education, and other aspects of secular life. However, over the last century, many Baptists abandoned separatism and were involved in secular activities. This shift was the driving reason behind the formation of the IFB movement: while other Baptists began voting, attending movies, and dancing, the independent Fundamentalists tightened their grip. Despite claiming sole possession of the true faith, the IFBs lately had their own problems with breakaway believers who believed the IFBs were too liberal and formed the New Independent Fundamentalist Baptist movement.

In reality, the New IFB members may be on to something. During the 1980s, the IFB, like other very conservative churches, began to flirt with outsiders, particularly in the political world. This was the time when Baptist televangelist Jerry Falwell established his Moral Majority movement to support Republicans. I wasn't aware of this trend, but political campaigns had captivated me in the same way that a toddler could be captivated by an all-action TV show. During the brief years my family resided in Jacksonville, Florida (my father worked in the shipyard), I became interested in a Democrat named John Lewis' mayoral run. Lewis, a young and enthusiastic state politician who resembled George W. Bush, was a rising star whose mainstream ideas made him a very effective state legislator. He attended our church, and his hot-pink yard signs wowed me. Lewis was defeated in the primary election. His failure was devastating to me. I answered by attempting to understand more about the workings of politics. I started looking for newspaper stories in which I might comprehend what each party stood for. And, like so many other kids born in the late 1970s, I looked up to Ronald Reagan as my role model for a successful politician.

Reagan was clever in collaborating with Christian Right leaders while maintaining the conventional Republicanism that appealed to the bulk of GOP voters. Despite Falwell's efforts to rally voters for Reagan and others, he was unable to achieve his supporters' main goals, which included a return to public school prayer, a ban on all abortions, outright dismantling of the US Department of Education, and significant rollbacks in environmental protection laws. As it became evident that Reagan had given Falwell little and gotten a lot, the Lynchburg, Virginia, preacher's political momentum dwindled. The initial Christian Right movement was a failure. However, a new movement had arisen in the tradition of very conservative churches. Pat Robertson, Falwell's adversary, established a more disciplined and "worldly" political organisation. The Christian Coalition was his idea. I was there when it hit the big time in 1992. I'd already noticed the disconnect between what too many Christians say and what they practise thanks to the short pants (avert your eyes!) and "son of a biscuit" (cover your ears!) occurrences. Nobody is flawless. That seemed obvious to me. However, the more insistent you are on your own perfection, the more hypocritical you appear when you are exposed to less than. This was never more evident than in the notion of separation. Groups that consider themselves superior to others and attempt to isolate themselves from the outside world resemble cults, and cults nearly invariably fail.

My parents, especially my father, were always interested in politics, despite its outside-the-world status, and were never dedicated to a holier-than-thou view of life. Of course, his faith informed his political ideals, which piqued his interest when he heard pals John Parrott and Lee Newcom discuss the Christian Coalition. They were the leaders of our local county Republican Party, as well as the state section of the Christian Coalition. They were decades ahead of their time.

My father took me to the coalition's national meeting in Virginia Beach when I was fourteen. It was 1992, and, unlike Falwell's Moral Majority, Robertson's alliance was not interested in assisting the Republican Party. It aimed to seize control before the next presidential election. With a lot of money and the media power of Pat Robertson's Christian Broadcasting Network, they were able to get seats at the Republican National Convention. This success and potential power had drawn President George H. W. Bush to the event, which looked very much like a political rally, from its "Road to Victory" theme to its patriotic decorations.

Bush had resisted the Christian Right's most extreme demands, such as the resumption of prayer in public schools, in 1988. He was the dog, and he wasn't about to let them turn into the tail that took over. However, in 1992, he understood that he needed conservative Christians to defeat an opponent, Bill Clinton, who was far more skilled and appealing to swing voters than Michael Dukakis. Bush was still unlikely to give the Christian Coalition more than lip service, but he couldn't turn down the invitation.

Bush declared common cause with the coalition during the 1992 convention, but he wavered in telling ways. He claimed he supported American families but did not want to "return to the days of Ozzie and Harriet," despite the fact that most people there sought the life depicted on that 1950s TV show. He mentioned linking America more closely to the rest of the world, which the audience found suspicious. They also knew he had been an Episcopalian his entire life, making him a liberal Christian.

At the time, I didn't comprehend the subtle differences between the Christian Coalition and the president. I was more interested in the atmosphere, the several speakers' speeches, and the reporters and TV crews working the fringes of the throng of perhaps a thousand people. My father and I had gotten front-row tickets by some miracle, and one of the teams came to the front of the room and focused immediately on us. We ended up on the CNN broadcast, which was the dominating 24-hour news channel at the time.

Nobody in the convention hall seemed concerned about the possibility of a religious organisation seizing control of one of the country's two major political parties. First, they were those who felt that America was a Christian nation, chosen by God to be the world's saviour. Politics would be a means of breaking Satan's wicked grip on their countrymen and becoming a spiritual beacon to the rest of the globe. They also thought the concept of church-state separation was incorrect. Conservative Christians once valued this concept because they were concerned about the state's influence on churches. They are now opposing it in order to wield control over the state. Finally, there was a widespread perception that they were losing social and political standing as a result of imminent demographic change—immigration and a fall in church membership—and that time was running out to do something about it. Urgency has long been a crucial component of conservative Christianity, which explains the many references to end-of-the-world prophecy made by preachers and the enormous popularity of so-called End Times publications. The Left Behind series by Rev. Tim LaHaye and Jerry B. Jenkins, the most popular of these novels, outsold most of the secular works that made The New York Times bestseller list. After centuries of hearing the phrase "the end is near," it has lost much of its power to elicit enthusiasm and urgency. Instead, the Christian Coalition said that godless leftists are on their way to destroy your marriage, family, church, and country. Robertson stated shortly after the convention that feminists want women to "leave their husbands, kill their children, practice witchcraft, destroy capitalism, and become lesbians." Nothing would move conservative Christians to action more than this.

In the end, the coalition's 1992 strategy failed, as did its attempt to seize control of the GOP right away. President Bush, on the other hand, had created the first overt link between traditional and even blueblood Republicans and conservative Christian activists with his visit to Virginia Beach. President George W. Bush, a true born-again Christian, would form a stronger bond with him. Bush's personal faith was soft, but he allowed his political team to exploit some of the Christian Right's deepest worries by supporting state referendums on gay marriage to increase turnout that would help their man.

Although I didn't realise it for many years, the vocabulary of power-seeking political conservatives began to fuse with the religiously conservative viewpoint to define the opposition as dangerous, anti-American, anti-Christian, perverted, and, eventually, wicked. An early example of this forceful spiritual language can be seen in Pat Buchanan's speech to the Republican National Convention in 1992. He warned of a "war for the soul of America" against "radical feminism," "homosexual rights," and "discrimination against religious schools" as a Christian Right stalwart who attempted to replace Bush as the GOP presidential nominee. Buchanan was often chastised for being too extreme, but on the outskirts of this intertwined religious and political movement lurked a more radical element: conspiracy believers. These people were the forerunners of the QAnon movement.

If you find it difficult to accept Christian conspiracists as related to today's plague of paranoia, consider that Pat Robertson publicly promoted the bizarre notion that a long-dead secret society called the Illuminati was conspiring with "atheists and Satanists" to control governments around the world in 1991, just before the Christian Coalition convention I attended. They could do so through important groups such as the Council on Foreign Relations, leveraging their connections to the financial world built by Jewish bankers. Their presence in the United States, he claimed, could be seen in dollar note symbolism, the mainstream media's role as Illuminati "propaganda" machines, and Bush's references to a "new world order." Bush stopped using this word on the recommendation of his Christian Right liaison because many religious conservatives mistook it for Satan's plan to take over the globe.

Republican rhetoric turned toxic as the old-school GOP aligned themselves with the movement Robertson started. Extremist figures rose to prominence as leaders of the faithful-political coalition. Outside of their culture war, their methods trumped policy considerations. This happened in such a subtle manner that few people, including me, realised what was going on. Instead, we went along for the ride where we could, ignored the rest, and failed to notice how our values were being replaced.

CHAPTER 2

POLITICS IN A BYGONE AGE

Consider the following headline for a newspaper: cordiality marks argument. Is it real or fake?

It's true, and it describes the first political debate I ever attended, hosted by the local League of Women Voters. The headline was followed by an article of my challenge to McLean County Board incumbent Allen Ware's attendance record in my hometown paper The Pantagraph (just next to a supermarket's ad for "Meat Mania"). He had responded by mentioning his family and the obligations of his career. Yes, he had skipped a few meetings, said Ware. But, like a student who misses a day of school, he was able to catch up on what had happened. And, he claimed, his time in office had made him familiar with every topic.

The year was 1998, and the date was October 22nd. Bloomington's Old Courthouse Museum served as the venue, with the largest courtroom serving as an auditorium. The courthouse was built in 1903, after a fire started in a laundry destroyed much of downtown. The Bloomington courthouse was built at a time when Midwest municipalities competed for civic architecture, and it was so attractive that it was eventually included on the National Register of Historic Places. This setting served as a timely reminder that we were participating in a timeless exercise in American democracy. I was twenty years old and still in college at the time. Despite my lack of experience, The Pantagraph—named after an old mechanism that makes a copy of a handwritten document—endorsed me the following day. The newspaper's encouragement helped to alleviate my fear of running. Eleven days later, I won the election by a vote of 1,725 to 1,580. It was a close call, but a win is a win. The county board post was not the type of high-level position that received a lot of attention on a daily basis. However, in 1999, national news had not yet begun to dominate the media, and McLean County residents were preoccupied with local issues. The Pantagraph's editors recognized this, which is why every week they produced a piece titled "New Names," in which all the infants born in its readership region were welcomed into the world. Those who graduated from high school received the same treatment, as the daily printed the names of everyone in its distribution region who received a diploma. This was once prevalent, but by the 1970s, most other tiny dailies had abandoned it. However, not ours. The Pantagraph treated me as if I had won the governor's race the day after the election, sending a writer to interview me for a front-page feature. They were reacting to the novelty of someone so young winning any election, not to the importance of my job. Of course, I answered the questions as if my victory was significant, because it was. I talked about accepting "all of the responsibility" and how I was "humbled" by the trust that had been placed in me. Strangely, my father's friend Lee Newcom, who was also a Republican, was swept out of his board seat by another newcomer in the same election, demonstrating the unpredictability of politics. But there was nothing unexpected about the way Allen Ware and I had handled ourselves. Although we referred to it as neighbourliness, cordiality and decency were a way of life in our land, originating in the farmers' tradition of relying on one another for harvests. As a result, local office candidates did not sling mud or do opposition research to find unrelated flaws and incidents to throw at one another. Thank you, God. Thank God, I say, because I had lived so briefly that any examination of my past would have soon led to, say, age twelve, when I caused a minor seventh-grade controversy. We were researching America's first war in Iraq, precipitated by Saddam Hussein's attack on our ally Kuwait. I saw the girls in our class were impacted by hearing about neighbours who were deployed, as well as the anxiety and uncertainty faced by their families. I informed them that my brother, Nathan, was in Iraq, hoping to impress them. He was actually in high school, but no one thought to verify. The next thing I knew, the school administration had enrolled me in a support group for children whose family members were serving in the military. I went partly because I didn't know how to get out, and partly because, well, free donuts. Given the nature of seventh-grade deceptions, I adhered to my tale and continued to elaborate on it. I mentioned my brother getting injured in a skirmish in a distant section of Iraq. Then I informed him that he was receiving treatment in a military hospital. How did it all end? As it turned out, the tabloid published every name of a local who had been deployed. (There they go with their hyperlocal coverage again.) My classmates kept checking to see why my brother's name didn't appear. I stated I didn't know, but my father was upset. Eventually my teacher discovered the truth and told me she knew what I had done. It was discussed in a way that was quite painful for me, but my penalty was my own sense of embarrassment. My deceit was not revealed to my students, which means that some of them are only now becoming aware of it. Decades later, I apologise to everyone I offended for lying. Except for a few drinking episodes, the lessons of middle school helped me go through my public school education with minimal further difficulty. One resulted in my parents' car becoming trapped in the mud in a field. They were not delighted as nondrinkers, and they let me know. Fortunately, I had no more involvement with the legal system during my high school years.

My freshman year at Illinois State University in Bloomington was spent immersed in fraternity life. Was it similar to the film Animal House? Almost anything. My stay there includes streaking through Bloomington, being chased by cops, and being apprehended after losing my footing, falling, and tumbling down a hillside in a park. My freshman grade point average was 0.8. You have to try hard, but I had a foolproof method: ignore my studies. I was asked to quit the university once my grades were calculated.During my exile, I worked as the furniture "manager" at Kay's Merchandise, a struggling regional business on the verge of collapse. Kay's sold everything from diamond rings to toaster ovens in their shops. As the furniture manager, I spent my time rearranging sofas, tables, and chairs. The finest part of the job was working with the store manager's daughter, but he made sure she had nothing to do with me. I petitioned for readmission to the institution and was accepted on the condition that my grades improve drastically and promptly. They did, and they stayed high until I graduated. Meanwhile, I was elected to the county board and began to use the political and policy themes I had learned in political science studies. Nothing could have prepared me for a career in politics better.

The county board was an excellent location to learn about how most people, who are uninterested in politics, go about their daily lives. The board addressed ground-level issues ranging from law enforcement and courts to road upkeep. Every driver is concerned about highway maintenance, but this is especially true in a region like McLean County, which spans 1,183 square miles, an area larger than the state of Rhode Island. With a population of only 150,000 scattered individuals, we required a road network of more than 1,000 miles. These arteries connect farmers to shipping hubs, from which their harvests are transported throughout the country and around the world. Nothing is more essential to the country's economy, which is consistently listed as one of the top five maize and soybean producers in the country. When you include farms that specialise in other crops, cattle, and eggs, you get to $1 billion in sales by 2020. It wasn't all that long ago that much of America looked and felt like McLean County. Roughly one-third of Americans still lived in rural areas in the 1960s. This number fell as Big Ag consolidated farmlands, but many farm families relocated to smaller towns like Bloomington and Normal, rather than big cities. All of this information is based on trustworthy statistics, as is the reality that today's rural areas are socially distinct in many respects. Approximately 64% of people in rural areas identify as evangelical Christians, compared to 25% nationally. Rural communities have greater rates of gun ownership, significantly fewer persons from minority groups, and far fewer occurrences of violent crime than non-rural communities. The fear of crime, on the other hand, is greater. Although suspicion of "Big Government " and poverty has long been a feature of rural America, government spending in the form of farm subsidy programs designed to maintain the food supply steady is welcomed. Critics describe it as welfare, although it is more akin to a national security program. Nothing is more critical to a country's security and strength than a functioning food supply system capable of withstanding extreme price changes. More contentious is the maize and ethanol fuel subsidies, which was designed to assist this industry compete. It is still paying for nonfood production forty years later. In the year I joined the McLean County Board, multiple programs paid a record $23 billion to commodity farmers on a national scale. Our farmers became so important to the local economy as a result of the money coming to them that the board frequently considered them in its work, and they, in turn, had influence over politics at all levels. Farm subsidies were well above my pay grade on the county board, but that didn't imply the issues were straightforward. Lee Newcom had encouraged me to keep my mouth shut and my head down for the first year of my term in order to learn the job and demonstrate that I wasn't a young know-it-all. I went along with his advice. Then I began making modest proposals. One of the first suggested that meeting times be changed from 9:00 a.m. to 6:00 p.m. so that more members of the public could attend. This was a 13-5 loss. I'm not sure why, but it seemed to me that board members found 9:00 a.m. convenient. They had also always done things this way. And perhaps they didn't want too many people to show up because they would be unruly, demanding, or misread what was going on. This third explanation did not occur to me at the time, but it now appears to be a viable one.

In mid-January 2000, I put my neck out a second time when I signed up to be a delegate for Arizona senator John McCain in the 2000 Republican presidential primary. With no incumbent Republican president, no one had a grip on the nomination, and more than a dozen Republicans claimed they were seriously considering running in 1999. They ranged from the fiery culture fighter Pat Buchanan, who was so unpopular that he had no chance, to a mild-mannered former undersecretary of education with a name recognition score of almost zero. (This was Gary Bauer. Do you have no idea who he is? Look him up on the internet.) By mid-February, with five or six weeks until the Illinois primary, only McCain and Texas governor George W. Bush were running significant campaigns. Bush had started the year with a massive lead in the main public opinion polls. On the day I stated my support for McCain, Bush had 42 percent of the vote, while McCain had only 8 percent. Obviously, I wasn't rooting for the favoured. Instead, I chose McCain because of his military background—he was a Navy pilot and POW in Vietnam— and because he was independent-minded and so frank that the campaign bus he had been riding on since September was dubbed the Straight Talk Express. McCain was the type of guy who, when branded "misinformed" by a voter, responded, "No, you're misinformed." When asked why Congress had not addressed health care, he stated that "the Democrats are controlled by trial lawyers, and the Republicans are controlled by the big money of insurance companies." When another voter suggested that the US should cancel trade deals because his business needed protection, he responded, "I would do anything to help your company compete," but then added, "I cannot tell you I would protect your company... I am a free trader." All of this occurred in less than twenty-four hours, during a visit to

New Hampshire, site of the first and typically most crucial primary election. Historically, New Hampshire Republicans were thought to be open-minded and moderate. Their admiration for McCain's candour scored him a large win there, propelling him to a 92-61 lead in delegates by the end of week three of the primary season. However, Bush's supporters in South Carolina, where his campaign planned to build a "firewall," had dug into the gutter to find a line of attack. They claimed in fliers and phone calls that McCain fathered a child with a black prostitute while in New York City. McCain's nine-year-old daughter Bridget, who was born in India, was cited as proof. These Bush supporters manufactured enough doubt by exploiting a youngster and bringing together a trinity of prejudice—race, sex, and a large, evil northern city—to help their guy win by nearly 12 points. Although Bush campaign officials maintained the leaflets and calls had nothing to do with their national campaign and disavowed them, McCain's momentum was lost, and he withdrew on March 9. With the Sedona mountains behind him and his wife, Cindy, alongside him, he said his party should do more to appeal to moderate independent voters and accept his key themes. These had included campaign finance reforms to drastically decrease the influence of large businesses and unions, as well as a ban on most actions by outside groups like the ones in South Carolina that disseminated the misinformation. The only thing he specifically mentioned in Sedona was a change in the tax law "that benefits the powerful few at the expense of many." With many in the press reporting that McCain was still outraged by how his daughter was exploited in South Carolina, he admitted that Bush was likely to be the Republican nominee but hesitated from endorsing him or promising to work for him. He would only say, "I wish him well." I didn't hold it against him. In Illinois, I told the local paper that I expected McCain would withdraw the day before his announcement. As a self-professed political nerd, I had been keeping track of the delegate count, analysing the remaining states—most of which were Bush strongholds—and comparing the 2000 election to prior ones. I'd been studying election records since I was ten years old (much like other guys who kept baseball box scores), so McCain's chances were evident. I thought he'd pluck off a few states here and there, but he'd never win. I stated that I would support Bush while being proud of my earlier choice. When the Florida recount problem erupted, I was completely on my side and relieved that Bush had won. However, I wasn't aware of all the circumstances surrounding events such as the so-called Brooks Brothers brawl, which I later learned was planned by the renowned Roger Stone. And I was concerned that, for the first time in 112 years, the Electoral College vote gave the popular vote winner the victory. These Bush supporters manufactured enough doubt by exploiting a youngster and bringing together a trinity of prejudice—race, sex, and a large, evil northern city—to help their guy win by nearly 12 points. Although Bush campaign officials maintained the leaflets and calls had nothing to do with their national campaign and disavowed them, McCain's momentum was lost, and he withdrew on March 9. With the Sedona mountains behind him and his wife, Cindy, alongside him, he said his party should do more to appeal to moderate independent voters and accept his key themes. These had included campaign finance reforms to drastically decrease the influence of large businesses and unions, as well as a ban on most actions by outside groups like the ones in South Carolina that disseminated the misinformation. The only thing he specifically mentioned in Sedona was a change in the tax law "that benefits the powerful few at the expense of many." With many in the press reporting that McCain was still outraged by how his daughter was exploited in South Carolina, he admitted that Bush was likely to be the Republican nominee but hesitated from endorsing him or promising to work for him. He would only say, "I wish him well." I didn't hold it against him.

In Illinois, I told the local paper that I expected McCain would withdraw the day before his announcement. As a self-professed political nerd, I had been keeping track of the delegate count, analysing the remaining states—most of which were Bush strongholds—and comparing the 2000 election to prior ones. I'd been studying election records since I was ten years old (much like other guys who kept baseball box scores), so McCain's chances were evident. I thought he'd pluck off a few states here and there, but he'd never win. I stated that I would support Bush while being proud of my earlier choice. When the Florida recount problem erupted, I was completely on my side and relieved that Bush had won. However, I wasn't aware of all the circumstances surrounding events such as the so-called Brooks Brothers brawl, which I later learned was planned by the renowned Roger Stone. And I was concerned that, for the first time in 112 years, the Electoral College vote gave the popular vote winner the victory. As the primary election approached, supporters on both sides published letters in local newspapers and promoted their candidates to relatives and neighbours. This was before social media or even email lists were important. People paid great attention to letters to the editor since they were one of the best ways to communicate with a larger audience. Reporting and commentary in the Bloomington daily drew greater attention, and Brady once again had an advantage. For years, he had interacted with the local press, and journalists had come to view him as a dependable source. Brady's hand was clearly visible in a Pantagraph pundit's column titled no-show kinzinger missed out on opportunity. The story revolved around my father's failure to attend the Sangamon County GOP's Lincoln Day luncheon.

Even if they don't identify Sangamon County, most Americans are aware that Lincoln Day celebrations are a Republican tradition throughout Illinois. Because the county included the state capital, the luncheon drew a who's who of the party's officials. Brady did show up, and like everyone else, he went about trying to impress, well, other Republican leaders. If socialising with a gathering that contained possibly a handful of voters from his area was an opportunity to garner votes, then every checkout queue at a convenience shop was as well. Of course, a reporter living inside the bubble of state politics would regard the luncheon as extremely important.

The same pundit went after us on an issue we raised, supposedly because we weren't tough enough. Our attack was centred on a long-standing scheme that allowed state senators to provide scholarships to state colleges and institutions with no control or restrictions on who could apply. The columnist chastised us for not making something of Brady's once-four hundred-dollar donation to the child of a political ally. But my father's point was that he would refuse a privilege that everyone else would gladly take. There was no need to make a huge deal out of the $400 donated to some kid.

The most vehement critique we levelled at Brady concerned his life outside of politics as a real estate developer. "The choice is someone who farmed," my father, who grew up on a family farm, explained, "or someone who chose a profession of putting asphalt over farmland."

We knew that by the time my father threw that pretty light punch, a state university poll had put us considerably behind Brady. No one knew if it landed, but we did know we got the Chicago Tribune's editorial approval. According to the report, "Rus Kinzinger had neither the money nor the legislative experience of Brady but his understanding of state issues and his creative ideas for cutting waste suggest he wouldn't need much time to get up to speed." It was thrilling to see one of the country's largest and most powerful newspapers support my father. However, the voters headed to the polls.

Brady won the primary by a margin of 9,422-4,721. It may appear to be a small turnout for such an important contest, but party primaries often bring only the most ardent Republicans. Except in counties where the party had a barnburner of a contest, the total vote was similar. Democrats experienced the same scenario in their campaigns. When ours was finished, my father contacted Brady to thank him and told the press that as a total newbie, he was grateful for the assistance he had received. "We're disappointed but we aren't devastated," he said. "The people speak, and we go on with life as it is."

I believe my father was disappointed, and by election night, he had decided that the game wasn't for him. He was especially turned off by fund-raising, as indicated by the final campaign income count. Brady had raised over $175,000, compared to our total of about $50,000, thanks to assistance from large groups such as teachers' unions and many individuals who contributed thousands of dollars each. Nobody handed us anything more than $500. When you look at the timeline of our revenues, you can see that we started significantly behind Brady, as Brady raked in more than $75,000 during one reporting period when our manager's prayers went unanswered, compared to our $4,000. This was the surest way to lose an election in an era when money matters. This was mostly due to my father's inability to stomach approaching friends, neighbours, and politically engaged strangers alike for money.

As it occurred, events were pushing me to contemplate running for public office. I would run for county board again, but events were forcing me to withdraw from political politics as well. It would be one of the few life-altering choices I would make.

CHAPTER 3
LIFE GETS SERIOUS

The sky was a clear blue expanse with no clouds. The temperature was a comfortable 68 degrees. A mild breeze of around five miles per hour blew in from the west. It was, in other words, a wonderful morning for flying, and as I had recently purchased an old, slow Cessna 150, I was itching to take to the skies. Instead, I was going from my parents' house to my job at a tiny technology business across the street from the Bloomington airport in my red '92 Ford Escort. Because, well, I was twenty-three years old, the car radio was turned to the puerile, filthy, but nevertheless humorous Howard Stern Show. Stern, who was in the throes of his drug addiction, was discussing the nude model Pamela Anderson when he abruptly interrupted and remarked, "I'm sorry to interrupt the fun, but this is a breaking news story, a serious news story." A jet collided with the World Trade Center. "The World Trade Center has caught fire."

When the North and South towers of New York's World Trade Center were finished in 1971, they were the tallest buildings in the world, eclipsing the Empire State Building, which was only a subway trip away. For thirty years, the Towers have been worldwide known symbols of America's financial supremacy. Given its symbolic significance, Stern was correct to break the news of an aeroplane falling in Manhattan, striking the North Tower, and the tale captivated the cast for a brief while. One recalled a 1945 incident in which an Air Force pilot slammed into the Empire State Building while flying in zero visibility. (It was the last time an aeroplane crashed in Manhattan.) Someone else questioned aloud whether the collision was a terrorism strike. I had the same feeling when my often mind-numbing commute, with its stupid amusement, became overrun with portents of disaster, and Pamela Anderson's discourse became especially juvenile and exceedingly obscene. Stern's puzzled sidekicks briefly changed the subject while out of character because the show was supposed to be unapologetically edgy. Stern is a wise man, and he returned to the topic of the plane crash. The South Tower of the World Trade Center was then hit by a second jet plane. The crash was broadcast live by a news crew on the spot. "So, it's a terrorist attack," Stern remarked. "It's gotta be."

Stern talked in a way that reflected the feelings of millions of Americans as every television network began live coverage that would continue for more than a week. Many people would have agreed with him when he said, "It's war." No other country would have dared to commit such an act of war against the United States. This left just one suspect with the means and motivation to carry out the attacks: Osama bin Laden. Bin Laden, the leader of the terrorist Islamic network Al Qaeda, declared war on the United States in 1996. Most Americans were unlikely to have heard of him or Al Qaeda, but the assumption that the attack was linked to Middle Eastern terrorism sprung to many minds. Stern stated emphatically, "We gotta bomb the hell out of them."

When I arrived at the office, there was nothing but stillness. I knew everyone would be downstairs in the office gym, watching the building's single TV. As I joined them, it became evident that nothing would ever be the same again for a long time, if ever. Our country had been attacked, and every citizen had to assume that the immediate crisis would last until we knew exactly what had happened and the extent of our casualties. Others claimed that officials feared there were other targets, including Washington, DC, and that fighter aircraft were airborne and patrolling the skies as we watched the news provided as it happened by journalists who had rushed to cover the assaults in New York. A Boeing 757 smashed into the Pentagon at 9:37 a.m. At 9:45 a.m., the United States and Canada blocked North American airspace for the first time in history. The fourth hijacked plane then crashed into a field in Shanksville, Pennsylvania. The South Tower collapsed quickly at 9:59 a.m., with one level pancaking into the next as the 500,000-ton building crumbled in a cloud of dust and rubble that flowed down narrow alleys and coated everything in what appeared to be volcanic ash. The North Tower fell in a similar method in less than half an hour. There was no doubt that we were being subjected to the most devastating surprise attack on American soil since the Japanese struck Pearl Harbor on December 7, 1941. Anger and a desire for vengeance replaced the shock and anguish I had initially felt. We were the most powerful nation on the planet in every way— militarily, economically, politically, and morally. If this attack had been directed by any government, no matter how powerful, our response would have been enormously forceful and undoubtedly supported by a large portion of the globe. If the hijackings and crashes were the work of a terrorist organisation, retaliation would be even more difficult, because these organisations were dispersed in small cells and trained in secret, frequently moving inside ungoverned regions in countries such as Afghanistan, Somalia, and Yemen. But we didn't have a choice but to try. And we'll keep trying till we succeed. September 11th altered my life, but not in the way you might expect. It did not oblige me to enlist in the military because I had started the procedure nine months ago. It did, however, bring me to war and a far better appreciation for the US military, our country's place in the world, and how each of us can play a role in major events. Most of my preconceptions about my country's destiny evolved as the ramifications of 9/11 became clear. The United States appeared to be beyond the reach of adversary governments and terrorists planning huge casualty assaults. Our flaws had been exposed, and I was battling like hell. 9/11 seemed to me to be a wake-up call to men and women my age. I told a reporter called Karen Hansen, who wrote about the early aftermath of the attacks in The Pantagraph. "We're a generation that 's been spoon-fed to us," I went on to say. "We've had everything." I then told her that I believed we were facing a test of our principles that could be summed up in a single question: "Is it more important to get ahead, or is it more important to do what is right?"

I don't recall ever being interested in becoming a military pilot. When I was a kid, however, and asked how someone qualified, I was informed that you had to have a significant aptitude for maths and science, as well as the discipline to put those gifts into top grades. It would also be advantageous if you had graduated from the Air Force Academy. I was afflicted by the same self-doubts that everyone who isn't a narcissist is affected by back then—and occasionally ever since. Hearing that pilots had to excel in two subjects that were not my strong suits had disheartened me. I never even applied to the academy.

After some study, I discovered that my college degree qualified me to take the two specific tests required to apply for training to fly for the Air Force or the Air National Guard: one to determine my IQ and the other to test my flying ability. I aced both and began the application process for Officer Training School. I was still waiting after 9/11 when the press claimed that Americans were flooding recruiters with calls. Unfortunately, this zeal evaporated when President Bush encouraged the public to get back to normalcy. He claimed that if people "don't want to go shopping for their families... don't want to go about their ordinary daily routines," the terrorists will triumph. I understand he was concerned about the economy and may have believed the government would respond fast and effectively, but he made a mistake. He denied a country prepared to unify behind a cause a true chance to do so, and by 2005, the Army, for example, had gained only 75 people to its ranks. I got notice that someone had dropped out of a Wisconsin Air National Guard seat just as I received my report date for the Air Force Officer Training School. (The Air National Guard trains alongside the regular Air Force. I could apply to the Air Guard's 128th Refuelling Wing at Mitchell Field near Milwaukee and, if accepted, fly for a unit that had the same training and mission as the Air Force, as well as some benefits known only to insiders.)

Although you may believe that the Guard is less capable than the regular Air Force, this is not the case. Guard pilots fulfil the same responsibilities and fly the same aircraft as their Air Force counterparts, and when challenged, such as in mock dogfights, they usually come out on top. This is due to the fact that Guard pilots tend to be older, more experienced, and have greater flying time. Guard pilots can also work and further their professions while serving in their hometowns. Many work as commercial pilots, which maintains them in top flying condition. Air Force pilots are not permitted to work outside the military and are transferred every two or three years. Even people who enjoy travelling become tired of the transfers. I only had a few hours to put together and submit a lengthy application package that included several papers and supporting documentation when I inquired about the Wisconsin job on the day of the deadline. It was the fax era, so meeting the deadline was a bother, but I accomplished it and soon found I had gotten the job. I'd train to be an officer and eventually a pilot who could manage the refuelling jets, dubbed "flying gas stations" because they fill up other planes so they can stay in the air longer for a war operation or a long-distance flight. This is how the United States Air Force can reach every location on the planet in twenty-four hours or less. Later, at one of the several stages of pilot training, an instructor addressed a classroom full of hopefuls, "Who here is headed for a Guard unit?" There were only two of us who raised our hands. "Take a good look at them," the lecturer said. "They made the right decision."

Officer Training School accepts college graduates who are accepted into the pilot program and teaches them about military society, command, and leadership. Everyone who completes the course receives the rank of second lieutenant. Almost everyone who stays for twenty years retires as lieutenant colonels. However, while rank confers benefits, status, and duty, it has no effect on the most fundamental aspects of the military experience, which opened my eyes to what is actually a culture that every American should understand and cherish. Camaraderie, ethical standards, and education all work together to produce a unified and exceptionally capable fighting force.

After a few weeks of classroom and simulator training, we were ready to fly in the T-37s, often known as Tweets, which looked like planes on a carnival ride and were scrapped in 2007 after 53 years of service. They weighed less than several SUVs and were so compact that two could fit on a basketball court. A learner and an instructor may take control at any time in the cockpit, which was housed in a plexiglass dome. The forward wall, which was painted black and loaded with dials and switches, was framed in Air Force grey metal.

The T-37 was designed like a tank, despite its diminutive size. The ugly little monster was treasured by most military pilots as the first jet flown by a large percentage of them, from the ear-piercing whine at start-up to a landing that felt like riding a skateboard at 100 miles per hour. In the meantime, the plane possessed the highest g-force onset rate in the Air Force—so rapid that you had to fight the gravitational force not to black out. The cruise speed was 425 miles per hour, and the maximum altitude was 35,000 feet. Not bad for a ride designed to train folks who had only a few hours in a single-engine prop plane. The roar of the engines and the smell of jet fuel produce an incredible adrenaline boost the first time you stand next to the T-37s at start-up. The cacophony created when a dozen engines power up is characterised by aviation writer Budd Davisson as a "kerosene-burning siren," and the sound waves threaten to tear you apart. The exhaust's tremendous heat superheats the air, causing molecules to rise and then fall as they cool, creating a wavy, mirage look. For me, the sight and sound evoked both dread and excitement—the chance of vomiting was considerable, and we expected sauna conditions in the cockpit. No one who signs up for this type of training isn't excited to put on a parachute (in case ejection is necessary) and a helmet and take to the skies.

I came close but never puked, and I handled the jets admirably. Given that my single-propeller Cessna 150 had a top speed of 125 miles per hour and was easier to land than anything else flying, my experience with the T-37 was reassuring. It made me feel more mature and less self-conscious, as if I had both a natural aptitude and an acquired skill that enabled me to respond meaningfully to the attack on my country. However, I was not without flaws. I made blunders that were remedied by instructors, and I made a nearly deadly error on a solo flight. Remember how I said g-forces? On that flight, I performed a split S, which entails flying inverted and tugging toward the earth until you emerge right side up and 180 degrees opposite the direction. As you point to the ground, you gain airspeed, so start slowly, say at 150 miles per hour. I began off too fast, at 100 miles per hour. The g-force pressure squeezed the blood arteries that supply the brain. I started seeing stars and then experienced a brownout. I remembered being taught to take shallow breaths and strain every muscle from my toes to my chest in order to move blood back up to the heart. I followed the protocol, excited, and took control of the plane before it became a dagger pounded into the ground. Because they weren't closely monitoring my flight, no one on the ground knew what happened. Despite telling a few friends, no one in authority was aware of my close call. The military ethos of solidarity is a strong binder. It explains why combat soldiers frequently declare they fight for one another, and why no operation is more important than rescuing a missing soldier, airman, or sailor. It only fails in extreme instances or when people are under the influence of drugs and/or alcohol. This happened to me in Altus, Oklahoma, a run-down town where pilots learn to fly the KC-135 refuelling plane. This was the first time I flew a large aircraft with outstanding capabilities. The tanker measures 136 feet long and has a wingspan of around 131 feet. The pilot's seat is around 35 feet above the ground, which provides an unusual perspective. Any weekend flyer would be astounded by the KC-135's performance. Its four engines are so powerful that it can climb faster than many jet fighters, with a maximum airspeed of 500 miles per hour. It has a range of more than 11,000 miles on a single fill-up. Its roof is 50,000 feet above sea level, providing a stunning view of the earth's curvature. Although the KC-135 can transport goods and troops, I'd say that 90% of the plane's operations involve filling up other planes. For this purpose, the plane's tanks hold 100 tons of fuel. Refuelling entails a ballet performed by a $100 million aeroplane cruising six miles above the planet. The tail boom that carries the gas is less than fifty feet long, indicating how close the planes go while flying at exactly the same speed and compass points. Mishaps are uncommon, but the KC-135 can withstand a little bumping and shoving. For example, in 1970, an SR-71 espionage jet pitched up, collided with a tanker in the belly, and crashed after its pilots bailed out. The refueler made a safe landing. It took me a few weeks at Altus to get used to piloting such a large beast—think of the riders who fly the dragons in Game of Thrones—but soon I felt as at ease as I would behind the wheel of a car. Even in a large aircraft, a pilot can detect little variations in performance. You respond naturally, examine the data on the instruments, and make changes. The experience of developing this sixth sense and establishing trust in the KC-135 was yet another way in which the military assisted me in maturing. Add to that the trust that came with being trusted with the plane and the lives of my crew, and flight school made me feel competent in ways I'd never felt before. This compensated for the base's lifestyle and community. Without disrespect to the city or the people at the base, I have to say that when I wasn't flying, Altus Air Force Base was the most dull assignment I saw in over two decades of service. I'm not the only one that believes this. In military press polls, it consistently rates among the worst in airmen's minds, right with sites like Minot Air Force Base, where the average high temperature is 23 degrees for three months of the year. The terrain, in addition to the 98-degree average high temperature in July, contributes to the difficulty of life in Altus. The stark beauty of the Western prairie may appeal to some. I saw vast dust-blown acres as flat as the top of your dining table, interrupted only by rows of spindly skeletons that seemed to reach forever. For the thousand or so young men and women stationed there, the town itself provides little recreation. Drinking was their most favourite leisure activity, and all but one of the establishments were roughneck hangouts where the local cops knew the frequent brawlers by name. Fights were less common at the exception, at least within the establishment. Five of us pilot trainees exited the "good" bar, ready to stumble back, on the one memorable night I spent downtown. We couldn't help but observe a couple having sex in the bed of a pickup truck in the parking lot. One of my friends cracked a joke about it. In an instant, the man in the truck rushed up and onto the ground, demanding that we fight. When we declined to fight, the guy began shouting, and we realised he was high on meth. The Air Force, like any other community, has its share of drug users. It was a major issue in the next town, where hopelessness, tension, and boredom seemed to lead many people to use. After standing nose-to-nose with each of us, demanding that we beat him, the irate man grabbed one of the other pilots' hands and used it to hit himself. This sparked a lot of debate. While two of the trainees fled, three of us stayed and restrained the insane man until he calmed down sufficiently for us to let go. "I'm a crew chief, you assholes," he said as we walked away. I'm going to wreck your plane and cause you to crash."

Crashes, while extremely rare, do occur, and US warplanes are shot down during combat missions. Fighter pilots are especially vulnerable since they fly at lower altitudes and are thus vulnerable to common shoulder-fired surface-to-air missiles. Tankers, which can fly at altitudes of up to 35,000 feet, are considerably above the range of most ground-launched missiles. Indeed, high-flying targets can only be reached by the most powerful ground-launched missiles, which are only available to the most powerful state actors. The most well-known example of a high-altitude shootdown included a US spy plane flying to the edge of space and being hit by a Soviet surface-to-air missile. (The plane was one of the renowned U2s, which first flew in 1957 and are still in service today. Gary Francis Powers, the pilot of the downed plane, survived and was returned to the United States in exchange for a Soviet spy held by the American authorities. He died seventeen years later when a helicopter he was flying for a Los Angeles television station crashed.)

The U2 tragedy demonstrates that, thanks to ejection seats and parachutes, as well as the way aircraft are built, the chances of surviving a missile strike or a crippling mechanical malfunction are better than you might assume. But if you do survive and land in a conflict zone, it's up to you to find cover, obtain food and drink, and avoid or battle would-be captives. This is why everyone who flies goes through basic survival training, which familiarises you with the equipment carried on every combat operation as well as strategies for caring for yourself before aid arrives.

Every combat flight is equipped with a pistol, night-vision goggles, a flare, some form of blanket, small lights, supplies, bandages, a radio, a knife, and anything for igniting fires.

When I was assigned to a hazardous assignment in Iraq, I would undergo significantly more comprehensive (even terrifying) training. This course was held at Fairchild Air Force Base in Spokane's Survival, Evasion, Resistance, and Escape—SERE—school.

We taught everything from how to get out of handcuffs to how to communicate with others if you are taken and imprisoned by the enemy during a week of classroom instruction.

The training's goal is not to teach participants how to avoid breaking. Everyone breaks, even if it's just a little, as individuals like John McCain learned while imprisoned in Vietnam. The shame that follows can last a lifetime and be more painful than any physical disability for those who believed it was possible to avoid it. Since Vietnam, the military has taught that during questioning, everyone reveals something. The best a prisoner can do is delay, limit their own damage, and try to reduce the value of what they say when they do start talking.

Even though I was nervously expecting the truly terrifying possibility of the wilderness simulation, I learnt a lot in class. When the time arrived, I joined a group of around a dozen cops who boarded buses that drove through the suburbs, small towns, and farmland to reach a mountainous wilderness. The group spent two days with an instructor who went above and beyond classroom lessons to teach us survival skills. He divided the group into three-person teams. Each unit was handed a map with a distinct location highlighted on it where we would meet our rescuers. Before taking off in the helicopter, the instructor warned, "The enemy will be looking for you." "Avoid getting caught." Because everyone gets caught, this training is more about applying what we've learned and controlling our fears and revulsions than it is about being out in the bush for an indefinite amount of time. For example, I've always had a profound dread of spiders but learned that I could handle them crawling all over me after a while. I also conquered my tenderness when I was tasked with slaughtering a rabbit for food, which was a chore that every tiny group had to complete. (Do not attempt this at home. Rabbits have a tendency to scream before they die.)

I was arrested, hooded, and bused over mountain roads to a rustic camp where we were interrogated by guys who appeared to be combatants for a fictional enemy nation days after our arrival in the bush. They were expert civilian contractors and military people who pretended to be either vicious bad men or seductive nice ones. The "commandant" of the camp was a sixtyish man with a large white beard whom we quickly began referring to as Santa Claus, but just among ourselves. We were exposed to repeated interrogations designed to prepare us for what we may face if we were apprehended in real life. I only got a few yells and threats. Instead, they tried to talk about my political interests, my bright future, and how if I simply talked to them, I could prevent myself from some major psychological suffering. I responded to the inquiries in a generic, diverting manner, including supplying "information" of little real worth, having been educated how to manage similar interrogations. Although I cannot go into great detail, SERE was not a pleasant experience. Humiliation played a significant role. For example, we were followed to every restroom visit and watched as we performed our duties. And anytime a cop arrived, we had to bend over, hold our ankles, and say out loud, "I hope you're having a great day, sir."

I was put in various stress positions and confined in spaces that would frighten anyone suffering from claustrophobia. Interrogators and torturers perform their dark arts in many prisoner of war camps where everyone can hear what's going on. This tactic is intended to increase feelings of worry, which it certainly does. Even though I understood it was all a sham, witnessing others go through intense confrontations affected me. The interrogators occasionally assaulted us with deafening sounds designed to confuse us. Consider hearing the sound of a baby weeping played backwards repeatedly. Another particularly frightening tape was an over-the-top reading of Rudyard Kipling's poem "Boots." The reedy audio is full of static, and Holmes' delivery is alarmingly monotonous, as recorded on a 78 in 1915 and now available on YouTube by an American actor named Taylor Holmes. It conveys, strangely, Kipling's perspective on a warrior's experience. You won't be able to understand it unless you know at least some of the words.

We're foot—slog—slog—slog—slogging' over Africa—

Foot—foot—foot—foot—slogging' over Africa—

(Boots—boots—boots—boots—moving' up and down again!)

There's no discharge in the war!

Seven—six—eleven—five—nine-an'-twenty mile to-day—

Four—eleven—seventeen—thirty-two the day before—

(Boots—boots—boots—boots—moving' up and down again!)

There's no discharge in the war!

Don't—don't—don't—don't—look at what's in front of you.

(Boots—boots—boots—boots—moving' up and' down again);

Men—men—men—men—men go mad with watchin' em,

An' there's no discharge in the war!

The recording was repeated so many times and so loudly that I imagined it as part of a program intended to drive someone insane. But it ultimately stopped, and so did the prison training. When Santa Claus passed me at a distance of around fifteen feet, I knew we were nearing the end of the day. "I hope you're having a great day, sir," I said through my legs as I stepped into the position. Santa came to a halt, approached where I was still hunched over, and said, "Son, you don't have to be so eager to do that."

Despite the fact that we had only been there for a week, the simulation had been so successful that most of us were relieved when it was finally finished. I, for one, fought to keep my emotions at bay.

Santa shook each of us hands after congratulating us on completing SERE. I grasped his hand tightly in a nonchalant manner, but a part of me wanted to beat the snot out of him.Some in our group did not attend the little ceremony that marked our departure from the camp. These handful had dropped out and would no longer be allowed to fly. Others, who persisted even as they went insane, did not resign, but were yanked out of the program by trainers who noticed they were struggling too hard. They were assured they will have another chance to try SERE. I'm sure they did because they wanted to finish what they started. This is the essence of the training received by our military men. A commitment to serve is matched by a commitment to provide the greatest possible assistance. anything your expertise, you will receive the best training available and will be prepared to deal with anything comes your way.

My preparation paid off about a year later, when I was strolling with several guys on a night out in Milwaukee while on active duty. A woman raced out of a pub, blood gushing from a gash in her neck, followed by a man with a knife, step by step. She screamed in the middle of the street, "He cut my throat, he cut my throat." We were close enough by this point that I was able to confront him, grab the wrist of the hand holding the knife, and twist him down to the pavement. I put my knee on his arm and avoided being knifed before the cops, who had been summoned by a witness, came with their patrol car lights flashing.

I climbed to my feet once the cops took control of the situation and felt the effects of the adrenaline—pounding heart, quick breathing, heightened senses—that had raced through my body as I struggled. I was likewise taken aback by my own behaviour. I was not the sort to fight. In truth, I had never been in a battle where I was in danger of receiving the kind of wounds that the irate, knife-wielding man could have inflicted on me. The key outcome was that the woman he had cut escaped and survived, and her assailant was unable to pursue anyone else.

The cops took my statement and photographed me before bidding me goodnight. I got in my car and drove back to my apartment complex while wearing a blood-splattered shirt. I was taken aback, but since there are no debriefings for civilians who intervene to prevent a violent crime, I would have to deal with it on my own. I dragged myself up to the fifteenth floor, entered the flat, and took off my shirt. I kept it in a corner of my bedroom for approximately a month before throwing it away for whatever reason.

This was a watershed point in my life. I demonstrated to myself that I possessed the skills and instincts to fight even when confronted with a major threat. I probably told the story best to Washington Examiner reporter Michael Warren: "I hear this commotion and screaming, and this girl is running at me across the street, and she's just holding her throat, with blood pouring out, I don't know if you've ever been in a situation where you've almost separated from your body, because it's just unreal,"

The slashing victim was being pursued by the perpetrator. With the knife still in his hand and a look on his face that could only be described as "psycho," I knew he'd kill her if he caught her. The only alternative was to charge at him, block him, and restrain him in some way.

I'd never fought someone who had the means and intent to murder me before. Survival tactics were taught to me in survival school. But something I learned in the Air Force had helped me maintain my cool. I had formed a mindset with the help of the trainers that allowed me to recognize danger and respond without hesitation. In an emergency, this is how pilots save themselves and their crews. It's also allegedly ideal practice for dealing with a psychopath wielding a knife.

The police record, which was discovered by a reporter, made the confrontation public. The Wisconsin Red Cross then presented him with a surprise "hero" award. Then I received the National Guard Valley Forge Cross for Heroism and the Air Force's Airman's Medal, which is given to service members who risk their lives for others outside of armed combat. It is infrequently awarded and ranks higher than the Bronze Star, which is awarded for battlefield valour. The president signs off on the award, which is signed by the secretary of the Air Force. It was presented to me during a ceremony in my unit.

It's unusual to get acknowledged for something I accomplished without much consideration. Leaving aside my heartfelt gratitude, I recognize that this type of award highlights the importance we place on behaving out of compassion for one another. Yes, the attention impacted me as a recipient, but I hoped that through the media accounts, others would be encouraged to take action if confronted with a similar circumstance.

CHAPTER 4

DEFEND YOUR COUNTRY, SEE THE WORLD

I had trained as a military pilot to fight in the War on Terror. By the time I was qualified, America had invaded Afghanistan, ousted Al Qaeda from its bases, and had eliminated its operational capability. The Taliban, the terrorists' backers, had been defeated, and a democratically elected government had been created in Kabul. The CIA and local security agents had apprehended the mastermind of 9/11, Khalid Sheikh Mohammed, in Pakistan. Our forces had overthrown Saddam Hussein in Iraq, paving the door for a new constitution and government. Saddam Hussein had been apprehended and was facing trial for mass murder. As eager as I was to help, the National Guard wasn't going to send me into war as soon as I acquired my wings. To be competent in battle, I needed to learn what it was like to function in unexpected environments. I saw my deployments as chances, learning as much as I could about local culture and history while opposing the typical lifestyle of military people on overseas deployment. Almost everyone on every post and base commutes between their jobs and the pubs that develop beside every American military site. Of course, I made those journeys on occasion. However, I made an effort to spend time with locals both on and off base, and if there were historic sites, I tried to visit all of the important ones. As I would later realise, America's global engagements—in trade, diplomacy, and defence—mean that people all around the world have preconceived notions about us. Some of these ideas are influenced by everything from movie fantasies (Rambo anyone?) to news about mass shootings to real-life contacts with Americans. You'd be shocked how many locals believe you're either CIA or a fantastically wealthy investment. These characteristics influence an adversary's spirit, civilian morale, and military leadership style. Consider how the Ukrainians reacted to Russia's invasion. This is not something you can learn overnight. However, even brief deployments abroad might serve as a reminder that knowing your adversary can save your life.

Many of the planes I would see in a variety of scenarios were refuelled during my operational training. No matter how many flights you fly, the start of the refuelling procedure always gives you a rush of adrenaline since we're doing this task so far above the ground. The massive transports glide up like warships, majestic and intimidating in size. Fighters frequently fly in formation, with left and right wingmates somewhat behind and to the side of the commander. While one hooks on and consumes fuel at a rate of 600 gallons per minute, the others wait to drop back when their turn comes. The training we provide is so good that after a few refuelings, pilots never appear to be frightened as they drive up to the pump, regardless of the type of plane they fly. In fact, they develop some insane abilities over time. Search for photographs of a camera crew standing in the open bay of a C-130 cargo plane to shoot a British Typhoon fighter to show what I mean. When they asked the pilot to get as close as possible, he nearly sank the Typhoon's nose into the harbour. This is the high-altitude equivalent of a fighter executing a stunt during an air show. That is very cool. However, this is clearly against the regulations. Those of us operating what is essentially a gigantic airborne gasoline bomb have our own set of skills and incredibly reliable equipment, especially for a jet that first flew in 1958. The manufacturer, Boeing, based it on their first airliner, the 707, which dominated the airline market with great engineering and construction. The KC-135s have been modernised, but some still fly with the original cockpit equipment, which makes getting into the driver's seat feel like stepping back in time. However, you can feel the sturdy construction. It is a safe and dependable aircraft, which explains why only five KC-135s have been lost in airborne incidents in the last 65 years. The only time I ever got into major problems while refuelling a jet was with a pilot attempting his first gas-up in a B-2 bomber, a stealth jet with a tailless wing that makes it extremely difficult to operate. It also costs a billion dollars every copy, which is why the US only has twenty of them. This one produced a bow wave, which is a key source of instability. I yelled, "Break away! Break away!" when I heard our boom guy key the mike and say, "Oh shit!" and we climbed out of the danger zone. My first deployments abroad took me to Latin America, Guam, and Turkey. In these locations, I would get experience similar to war-zone activities. Every foreign assignment, especially those near an adversary's border, increases the risk of an international crisis, putting additional pressure on every trip. We got some hands-on experience with history and geopolitics while we were there, which was intriguing to a policy nerd like myself. We took off from Andersen Air Force Base in Guam, one of fourteen full-scale sites operated by the United States on the Pacific Rim. The island, a tropical paradise, is 6,000 miles from the US mainland and is considered the most isolated sliver of US territory in the world. It also serves as a living museum. Archaeologists came to witness the three- to five-thousand-year-old pictographs discovered within a limestone cave by a population of farmers and fishermen who migrated from coastal China. They were known as Chamorros and lived in a class-based society ruled by women. The arrival of Ferdinand Magellan and his troops, who landed at a small bay on the island's southwest coast, was the Chamorros' first encounter with true strangers. They were determined to create a new westward route for trade between Europe and Asia. Their arrival in Guam is commemorated by a beachfront obelisk and plaque that make no mention of the indigenous people. "On March 6, 1521, Ferdinand Magellan landed near this location," it adds. Magellan had travelled for three months, believing that the Spice Islands (modern Indonesia) were a three-day sail from where he left at the tip of South America. He landed with a sick and weakened crew who had survived on rations for roughly a week and witnessed scores of their number starve to death. The Chamorros provided food and drink to the survivors before stealing things such as blades from the ships, presuming they were selling. Magellan deemed this stealing, and after they had recovered their health, he ordered his soldiers to slaughter and burn a handful of Chamorros. Guam and its archipelago were later dubbed the Islands of Thieves by the explorer. The tale of Magellan and the Chamorros is one of many examples in history of how individuals who don't understand each other might end up in catastrophic conflict. This is a challenge that invading countries have repeatedly experienced. This dynamic harmed the United States in Vietnam, Somalia, Iraq, and Afghanistan. We are not alone in this. The Soviet Union failed to learn their lesson in Afghanistan, and the Russian Federation has done so again in Ukraine. Hubris won the day for Magellan on his next trip after Guam, where he attempted to terrify the people of the Philippines with a display of contemporary cannon fire. They responded with a force of almost a thousand combatants, killing Magellan and driving his troops back to their ships. Visitors to Guam who are interested in military history will find that the Spanish returned to the island 150 years after Magellan to protect—what else?—trade. They constructed forts in harbours where galleons passing through the Pacific halted for supplies. (At sea, these ships were alone against pirates.) Madrid remained on Guam until the Spanish-American War ended, when they surrendered control of the island, as well as Puerto Rico and the Philippines, to the United States. They also relinquished their claim to Cuba, the starting point of the war, leaving it under American control as well.

After twenty years, the American military on Guam began a new conflict. As World War I raged in Europe, allies attacked German colonies and outposts in a 5,000-mile arc from the Marshall Islands to New Guinea, and then China. When a German gunboat dubbed the Cormoran II came to Guam in search of gasoline, the military governor refused to supply it and detained the crew. The governor then ordered the ship taken in America's first raid of the war after receiving word that the US had joined the war. The crew of the Cormoran II sank the ship. Seven members of the crew were killed in the battle and are remembered with a German-language headstone in an oceanfront cemetery where the six bodies recovered are buried beside American Marines and civilians. Despite its isolation and scant population, Guam's strategic location has kept it a critical military asset. Japan attacked and occupied the 200-square-mile island two days after the bombing of Pearl Harbor. Submarines from the United States harassed enemy ships off Guam until one of them entered the harbour and sank the troop carrier Tokai Maru. (It came to rest three yards from the keel of the on-side Cormoran II.) Guam was not liberated until 1944, after a fight that claimed the lives of about 1800 Americans and almost 20,000 Japanese. Shoichi Yokoi, a Japanese sergeant, hid in the jungle for twenty-six years after the war, hiding in a cave and hunting and collecting at night. Many believe he was unaware the war had ended. In reality, he had concealed himself to safeguard his honour. Visitors can visit all of these locations, from Magellan's landing site to the side-by-side graves of the two enemy ships to Shoichi Yokoi's hand-dug cave. In reality, the sunken warships attract over a thousand divers each year.

How many tourists are familiar with the entire military story and the lessons it may teach? Very few, most likely. Heck, I know that most troops are considerably more likely to attend one of the numerous strip clubs located within a minute's drive of both Andersen and Naval Base Guam. Those of us who rolled down the runway to take off over the 500-foot-high Anao Cliffs, on the other hand, were met with a sobering reminder of America at war. A submerged B-52 rests in the clear water just before the shore, visible from the air. Assigned to Operation Arc Light, a Vietnam War project that targeted the North's so-called Ho Chi Minh Trail, the jet suffered technical problems as it cleared the airport and crashed. The entire crew perished. Thirteen others died as a result of pilot mistake or mechanical failure. In one instance, two B-52 bombers collided in the air as they circled the skies, waiting for a KC-135 to refuel them. Furthermore, the North's anti-aircraft weapons supplied by the Soviet Union would drop eighteen B-52s. It's no surprise that many pilots feared the sorties to Vietnam, and that many more questioned Washington's determination to conduct the war in this manner. Andersen was a little tattered around the edges when we arrived in Guam in 2005. A drive down ArcLight Boulevard revealed a landscape covered with tall grass and weeds—how many young airmen realised why it had this name? Migrating birds flew down to eat on seeds and constructed nests near the runways. A B-52 pilot spotted a flock of birds as he rolled down the runway for takeoff in 2016. The drag shot that would have helped stop the massive airliner failed to deploy as he attempted to abort. The plane veered off the runway and caught fire. Although the crew was unharmed, the $112 million plane was destroyed. Our role would be to provide support to bombers and surveillance planes patrolling the coasts of North Korea and China. Both governments were no doubt upset by our flights and used radar to track us. This response came at a cost because it enabled us to identify their air defence systems. The Chinese, like the Russians, would occasionally scramble fighter jets to tail American patrols. After a catastrophe in the air over the South China Sea in 2001, they reduced the number of challenges and ceased endangering our aircraft with dangerous manoeuvres.

Two Chinese fighter aircraft flew out to meet a Navy EP-3 observation plane in that encounter. These aircraft, which are powered by four propellers and have a cruising speed of 200 miles per hour, are loaded with technology that intercepts and records signals. An aircrew of three sat in the front row, while twenty-one professionally qualified people—including cryptologists, linguists, and technicians—monitored the equipment. One of the Chinese fighters conducted a couple of passes close to the EP-3. The pilot realised he was about to collide with the slow-moving American plane on his third approach. He did not correct it in time. When the fighter collided with the outer propeller on the EP-3's left wing, the blade sliced the fuselage in half, sending the cockpit cartwheeling upward. As the cockpit shattered, the pilot ejected and plunged toward the South China Sea. The damaged EP-3 fell onto its back and plummeted from eighteen thousand feet to around four thousand feet. The pilot eventually got it right and was flying level. They were allowed to land at a Chinese facility on the island of Hainan after declaring an emergency. Despite the fact that the Americans were able to destroy some data while in the air, they were pushed out of the plane shortly after it came to a stop. The Chinese received a cache of encryption codes, surveillance manuals, technological secrets, the names of US spies, and huge volumes of data gathered from our rivals around the world. The Americans were released after ten days, but the Chinese remained in possession of the plane for months. This was one of the worst losses of secrets and specialised technologies in history. Stories of what may go wrong on military operations are more than just dramatic morsels of history to spice up a bar stool chat or a book. They serve as regular reminders that in every flight, both human lives and national interests are at stake, whether it's a training exercise in the United States or electronic surveillance on a geopolitical competitor. We focused on our work during our surveillance trips, knowing that an emergency may happen at any time. We operated in Turkey from the NATO base at Incirlik, which is roughly 25 kilometres from the Mediterranean. This was yet another location that had begun to deteriorate but was reviving in order to support the operations in Iraq and Afghanistan. On our off evenings, we would go out and investigate abandoned facilities, such as a base housing area that felt a little like a little town during 1985 that had been abruptly abandoned by every townsperson. The structures were Cold War antiques from a time when Turkey was part of the bulwark that kept the Soviet Union at bay, much to Moscow's chagrin. The most memorable chapter in US-Turkey relations happened in 1962, when the Soviets attempted to breach our defensive line by stationing nuclear-tipped missiles in Cuba. President John F. Kennedy declared war, and the United States military was placed on high alert, keeping B-52s constantly armed and manned for takeoff. When Moscow surrendered, Kennedy handed the USSR the face-saving gift of removing fifteen outmoded nuclear weapons from Turkey—"those friggin' missiles," Kennedy termed them. The Turks, who were opposed to the relocation, would soon receive improved nuclear security from bombers stationed there, although this was done secretly. In addition to military spending, it received international aid. Turkey's engagement in cooperative anti-terrorism operations began 44 years ago, following 9/11, when it was one of the first countries to offer condolences and volunteer to join the American-led War on Terror. Turkey's assistance included the use of the Incirlik base by the allies, which was critical for transferring supplies, ammunition, and manpower to both Iraq and Afghanistan, as well as unfettered passage through their skies for any aircraft heading to conflict zones. The Turkish government also surreptitiously shared a lot of intelligence based on its well-developed spies network and capacity to intercept and analyse conversations. Planes transporting Al Qaeda terrorists captured on Afghan battlefields were refuelled in Turkey, and this level of cooperation occurred despite the fact that it annoyed other Muslim-majority countries. The Turkish people, for the most part, appeared to support their country's position in the global anti-terrorism campaign, as did people in the majority of the countries that had joined the effort. For the KC-135 crews who were rotated in and out of Incirlik, our task had become regular. We normally took out at night and flew 350 miles across the nation to the Black Sea coast, then to a certain area of the sky known as an "anchor" or "box." We flew in predetermined patterns, waiting for one of the large C-5 and C-17 carriers flying to Iraq from Europe to appear out of the darkness—imagine a massive shark suddenly appearing in a black ocean.

The C-17s are large enough to transport war vehicles such as tanks. The larger C-5 is such a beast that airmen refer to it as the FRED, which stands for Fucking Ridiculous Economic Disaster. It's amusing, but it's also incorrect. No other plane can feed a ground force as efficiently as the F-16. It can operate in severe situations, including dusty dirt airfields. Many C-17s have continued flying for more than thirty years, despite being built at a fraction of the cost of a B-2 or an F-22 Raptor. The environmental record is more difficult to analyse, however given that the US military is the world's single largest consumer of fuel, the C-5 accounts for a very small percentage of the total. Despite the fact that US planes flew over Turkey virtually every day, most Turks never saw us. Most of my missions were at night, and we were back at Incirlik before the rest of Turkey woke up. On our few daytime missions, we followed the guidelines for making as little noise as possible and flew so high in the sky that you had to know we were up there to spot us. We were pleased to be a part of an anti-terrorism program that was, by all accounts, succeeding. We had brought lethal accountability to Al Qaeda and its defenders in Afghanistan, and we had apprehended other terrible men from around the world. Yes, the mistakes in the assessment that led to our invasion of Iraq had sparked a growing controversy. However, that war had attracted terrorists, whom we were able to combat there. In addition, our success in combating Islamic terrorism was evident. There had been no further successful strikes on the United States. France, Germany, Italy, Denmark, Canada, Belgium, Poland, Turkey, and other NATO allies were also spared devastating strikes. Tragically, both Spain and the United Kingdom had multiple mass-casualty events on the same day. In total, 249 persons were slain. Nobody should downplay the magnitude of these atrocities. In the following decade, however, only one person, a soldier, would be killed by an Islamic extremist in the United Kingdom. Spain would be free of fatalities for an even longer length of time. It's impossible to estimate how many conspiracies were foiled over that time period. At least thirty large planned attacks, however, were thwarted. Given Turkey's proximity to terrorist-producing countries—Iraq, Afghanistan, Syria, and Iran—its experience was remarkable. Indeed, as the Cold War gave place to the War on Terror, America maintained a significant role in ensuring its security. The US also gave economic assistance. Defence and dollars combined to provide American presidents decisive leverage with governments all over the world. Today, we provide security for half of the world's population and are primarily responsible for maintaining trade routes open for the entire planet. These missions explain why every branch of the military, including the Coast Guard, maintains significant foreign bases. Indeed, if you include little outposts, we have approximately 750 international locations.

My time in Turkey proved to be an ideal opportunity to learn about the country's political and strategic significance. Bilateral ties remained on the course established immediately after World War II. Turkey's democracy has long served as a model for the Muslim world. Women and ethnic minorities were gaining equality, and Islamic extremism had been unable to establish itself. Prime Minister Recep Erdogan, who was committed to joining the European Union at the time, had even begun negotiating with Turkey's large Kurdish population—roughly thirty million—part of a community of fifty million who considered the region where Turkey, Iran, Iraq, and Syria met their native land. They shared an indigenous culture and a desire to right an injustice done to them at the close of World War I, no matter where they resided. The allies promised them a state at the time, only to back out three years later. Since then, their desire for liberty has piqued the interest of many in the American foreign policy establishment. They felt even more deserved when they became our allies following 9/11. Given my intense interest in global affairs and military policy, I devoured information on both the past and current situation of Turkish-American relations. Although I had quietly hoped to become involved in the American side of international issues, I had no idea I would eventually become one of those in the US government who supported the Kurds out of respect for the blood they shed with us in Iraq and their insatiable desire for self-determination. It became evident to me that in our relationship with Turkey, we should use the normal carrots and sticks to push Erdogan to provide more autonomy to the Kurds. We would owe the Kurds even more after they fought and died alongside us in the successful battle that took down the mediaeval "caliphate" formed in Syria and Iraq by a ruthless terror organisation known as ISIS from 2014 to 2017. Any other American president would have honoured the Kurds by increasing our efforts to help them. Donald Trump, on the other hand, would not. In an episode I'll go into more detail about later, Trump backtracked on a pledge to defend Kurds who had escaped Turkish forces and sought safety in neighbouring Syria. He evacuated the American forces that were protecting the Kurds. Then Erdogan, whom Trump had previously referred to as his "favourite dictator," invaded Syria. As Turkish troops slaughtered Kurdish people, Trump said that the US had no interest in what he referred to as "a lot of sand." Erdogan's army would slaughter more than 200 Kurdish people. What action did Trump take after Erdogan defied him? He expanded Turkey's foreign aid to more than $200 million in domestic aid just before leaving office in 2020, more than tripling the amount donated in the previous decade. Why did Trump act in this manner? It could have been related to his declared admiration for strongmen—Erdogan, Kim Jong Un, Xi Jinping, Mohammed bin Salman, and Abdel Fattah al-Sisi—or to his business in Turkey, where he made $13 million for giving his name to a real estate project. His daughter Ivanka had persuaded the Turkish government to approve the building. She may want to try it again. In my third deployment outside of combat zones in Colombia, we refuelled planes looking for illegal coca farms and processing facilities, as well as elements of a rebel force that had originated in 1964, I kid you not. This army, known as the Fuerzas Armadas Revolucionarias de Colombia (FARC), was funded by kidnapping and ransom demands, as well as taxing coca producers and processors in the areas they controlled. The FARC was not a motley bunch of idealistic liberation fighters. They were fervent Marxists who intimidated innocent people. When I came, they had just perpetrated mass murders and had been denounced by the United Nations.

When the FARC wasn't executing Colombian soldiers and locals, they were kidnapping people and demanding ransoms. Thousands of people have been kidnapped and detained. Most were detained in very reasonable conditions for short periods of time before being freed when the FARC received ransom payments of a few thousand dollars per individual. The guerillas, on the other hand, requested up to $1 million for high-profile detainees. When they did not get the money, the hostages were subjected to atrocities. Some were shackled to trees while others were ill from starvation after being denied food, shelter, medical attention, and clothing on a regular basis. All were compelled to take part in frequent long marches through the jungle in order to avoid being discovered by searchers.

Three Americans, Thomas Howes, Keith Stansell, and Marc Gonsalves, were detained by the FARC in 2003 when their jet crashed into a tropical jungle the size of California while on a joint surveillance mission with the Colombian military. A tenth of the region had been abandoned by the Colombian government and was being controlled as a kind of country inside a country by the guerillas. Vehicles could only travel on two two-lane roads in this area. People travelled along pathways or in small boats that sailed muddy waterways elsewhere. FARC combatants, who had grown up in the area, were significantly more familiar with the environment and landscape than military personnel. This meant that the army had to rely on a lucky break or a FARC blunder to discover a camp location, which nearly never happened. Meanwhile, the information provided to detainees' families was often limited to images of a loved one clutching a current newspaper as proof of life.

The more harsh measures were most likely a desperate reaction to Plan Colombia, a massive Colombian-American security and social program offensive. Plan Colombia, which began in 2000 during the Clinton administration and was funded with $10 billion, was more than just spending money to combat the FARC and feed the poor. The anti drug component of the program increased attempts to destroy the coca crop while assisting farmers in growing legal income crops and bringing them to market. America insisted on investing $20 million per year in reforming civil institutions such as courts and law enforcement organisations. Corruption in Colombia's government at all levels was apparent and had a significant role in rural support for the FARC.

Under President George W. Bush, Plan Colombia was expanded to include an attack on a growing heroin trade (some growers having shifted from coca to poppies). Contrary to popular belief, the campaign was successful in reducing the amount of land dedicated to cultivating narcotic crops and destroying an increasing number of processing facilities each year. The amount of coca recovered by police had increased dramatically, and the estimated output of cocaine had dropped off a cliff within a year. In the years that followed, progress was less dramatic, and the bad guys made their own successes for brief periods. However, the general trends remained good long beyond 2010. The civic society changes resulted in a two-thirds decrease in killings and an even bigger decrease in kidnappings.

The program's success confirmed that the United States was still the "indispensable nation" when it came to dealing with severe world concerns. With the end of the Cold War and the fall of communism (even China and Cuba were reforming), people all over the world were looking for the same freedom, peace, and stability that we had. So many countries sought our guidance and assistance that it appeared, at the moment, that we would lead a worldwide push toward democracy. However, one of the other foreign policy factors that becomes evident while spending time in Latin America is that we also tend to embrace authoritarians when it serves our interests. People remember how we supported leaders like these in Panama, El Salvador, and Nicaragua. This makes our efforts to promote democracy much more difficult.

Unfortunately, a subset of American citizens has always been isolationist or anti-interventionist, believing that we could safely ignore the rest of the world. This theory piqued the interest of some even after 9/11, when polls revealed that as many as half of Americans believed conspiracy theories regarding the attacks. These "truthers" were led by figures like radio host Alex Jones, who claimed that the events of 9/11 were organised by a strong cabal intent on building a "new world order" that would replace sovereign states with a single authority. Participating in a worldwide anti-terrorism effort would only help the scheme. Conspiracy theories are the extreme end point of an argument that begins with complaints about spending money elsewhere rather than at home—though this is a flawed argument because we benefit strategically and economically from military and development aid. When it came to the illicit drug trade, the dark fantasies included: President Nixon launched the War on Drugs in order to imprison Black voters; the CIA caused a surge of addiction by shipping cocaine to urban areas; and harsh sentencing laws for drug crimes were designed to load prisons with Black males. It is incredibly difficult to debunk conspiracy theories, especially when they involve national security or high levels of government. (Keep in mind that millions of Americans believe the first moon landing, Apollo 11, was staged more than fifty years ago.) When the sources of the conspiracy theories are considered, they appear less compelling. They include overzealous journalists and activists who believed they had legitimate claims to make, as well as former authorities with questionable motives. For example, John Ehrlichman, Nixon's counsel who was imprisoned following the Watergate affair, may have tried to damage Nixon by accusing him of implementing a racist strategy. In truth, there is no proof that Nixon intended to suppress the Black vote through drug charges. Similarly, only circumstantial evidence supports the accusation that the CIA caused the inner-city drug issue. And, while harsh sentencing policies did disproportionately harm minority populations, this was an unintended consequence of the laws, not an intended result.

My stance on drug policy was fairly conservative, and I was confident that, with the exception of occasional political grandstanding, most government leaders were truly worried about the impacts of illegal drugs. In the late 1980s, media coverage of drug misuse was so intense—a crack cocaine "epidemic" overblown beyond reality—that pollsters discovered in 1989 that 64 percent of Americans thought drugs to be the country's most serious problem. No other issue had ever received such a high rating. Lawmakers reacted to voters with ideas they believed would be beneficial. However, as the press calmed down and drug usage ceased to be a major public concern, official concern remained. So was the legislation that resulted in a genuinely astounding increase in incarceration—from less than four per thousand men in 1985 to nearly 10 when I visited Colombia. I'd been taught since first grade that drugs were a serious threat and that our efforts were required. I first heard First Lady Nancy Reagan's "Just say no" message. Then, in sixth grade, daytime television began airing commercials featuring an egg fried in a cast-iron pan and a voiceover proclaiming, "This is your brain on drugs." I had gone to D.A.R.E. (Drug Abuse Resistance Education) classes at school, as did almost every other student. Then there were the drug alerts at church, and then there were all the messages from my relatives. (I trusted these authorities despite the fact that, in an ironic twist, the D.A.R.E. an officer who visited my sixth-grade classroom was caught and legally charged with—yep—drug possession.)

I embraced the opportunity to participate in Plan Colombia because of my concern about America's drug problems and my desire for an alliance that would make Colombia a part of America's world. It was just another example of how our interaction and cooperation with other countries strengthens our global standing. Add in our military's response to natural disasters, and people all over the world regard our engineers, aviators, search-and-rescue workers, and regular troops who transport lifesaving supplies as heroes. Learning about our global effect and comparing it to people's sentiments at home will be beneficial in my future political career. But at the moment, I merely filed away what I saw and heard and looked forward to future deployments where I might fulfil the purpose that drew me in. To be candid, I wanted to join the struggle after leaving my home and family and waiting for years.

CHAPTER 5

LESSONS OF WAR

At 30,000 feet, the landscape of conflict can resemble the landscape of calm. When I first started flying tanker missions in Iraq in 2005, it was a place of lightly frequented two-lane roads slicing across large areas of brown and rust-coloured desert. Green farms lined the banks of the Tigris and Euphrates rivers. Sun-baked communities in peace. It was difficult to tell from the windows of our plane that people were fighting and dying on the ground. You couldn't detect the mounting terror and pessimism among ordinary Iraqis, or that a burgeoning insurgency fueled by Islamic extremism was dragging the US forces into a quagmire. The stalemate of 2005 would have been unthinkable in the early days of the war, when the American-led coalition army launched a now-famous four-day bombardment—dubbed "shock and awe" by commanders—followed by a "running start" attack by ground forces. Our armoured divisions and troops, which had gathered in adjacent Kuwait, advanced at such a breakneck rate that the opposition was thrown off guard. Officers lost communication with troops, and the troops were so disoriented that many of them abandoned their posts, preferring to surrender or return home rather than face the attack. Baghdad fell in less than three weeks. Three weeks later, President Bush landed on a seaplane to deliver a stirring speech in front of a banner that read "Mission Accomplished."

This joy concealed the mounting evidence that the Iraq war was authorised on the basis of poor intelligence. Iraqis did not aid the 9/11 hijackers, as officials initially suspected, and, while Saddam Hussein muddled the situation, his soldiers lacked weapons of immense destruction. The Bush administration gave these two grounds for war, but by the time he announced the start of the invasion, the president had stopped implying a link between Iraq and 9/11. Instead, he only spoke of freeing the Iraqi people from the authority of strongman Saddam Hussein and defending the world from "an outlaw regime that threatens the peace with weapons of mass murder."

This declaration of "Mission Accomplished" would prove premature as a strong insurgency of Islamic extremists and former members of Saddam's military grew to wage war against the allies. They planted thousands of improvised explosive devices (IEDs) throughout the highways, and soldiers were killed or injured when their vehicles collided with them. They also carried out direct strikes that grew increasingly daring and ambitious. Thousands of rebels engaged US forces in two battles over Fallujah in 2004. Ten weeks of fighting killed 122 Americans, and while it was hardly a defeat, Fallujah made many people back home understand that the war was not going as well as they thought. If more individuals had had direct touch with those who served, Americans would have been better informed about the realities of the war. In actuality, only around seven tenths of a percent of Americans served in the military, and everyone else, outside of their friends and families, had heeded President Bush's advice to live their lives as if 9/11 had never happened. It was widely assumed that this would demonstrate that the terrorists had failed, and it did have the added virtue of averting the economic disaster that would have occurred if people had continued to work and live as before. This business-as-usual approach mirrored a statement made to a reporter by a high-ranking Bush official two years into the fighting: "We're an empire now, and when we act, we create our own reality." And while you're studying that reality prudently, we'll act again, producing new realities for you to study as well, and that's how things will work out." The same journalist that broke the empire remark published an on-the-record statement from former Reagan administration official Bruce Bartlett, who prophesied that if Bush won reelection in 2004, regardless of Iraq, "there will be a civil war in the Republican Party." This battle, which occurred after Bush was re-elected, pitted extremely conservative, faith-based Republicans against typical policy-oriented Republicans. Bush would be in charge of the religious side. "He truly believes he's on a mission from God," Bartlett explained. "Absolute faith like that trumps the need for analysis." Faith is all about believing things for which there is no empirical evidence." "But you can't run the world on faith," Bartlett hesitated before adding, "But you can't run the world on faith."

Officers at other bases recognized that a little wiggle room is good for morale, so they let most minor violations slip. The commander at

Al Udeid was unusual. He kept a tiny army of enlisted men and women—the type who would have been junior high hall monitors—to enforce the belt requirement, T-shirt standard, and other standards. I was once caught in the chow hall wearing something that wasn't allowed. I showed the soldier that I was tired of the rules—or, to be more specific, I reminded him that I outranked him. He dashed off to collect an officer who outranked me, leaving me with little choice but to comply. If I could go back in time with my current rank of lieutenant colonel, I'd fire half of those monitors and everyone involved in creating the stupid regulations. While the uniform narcs were infuriating, the personnel that assisted with our refuelling trip were excellent. Maintenance personnel kept the vintage planes in great condition, and those in charge on the ground worked with the perfect balance of efficiency and caution. The primary threat to military fliers leaving the Al Udeid bubble occurred during takeoff and landing, and involved industrial-calibre lasers flashed from the ground, which could produce blinding light inside a cockpit. When the harassment started, local authorities worried if it was a low-level hostile attack. However, this explanation was rejected in favour of the belief that it was simply a case of jackassery. These gadgets were being shone at planes by idiots all over the world. Some of those apprehended claimed to have only wanted to see whether they could strike a jet with their beams. Others desired to experience the power of compelling a pilot to react. Fortunately, the likelihood of a catastrophic mishap was low, but as a precaution, we were compelled to wear uncomfortable and ridiculous-looking red goggles during takeoff and landing. We might hear ineffectual squawks from Iranians on an emergency frequency once we were in the air and above the Persian Gulf. "American aircraft at thirty thousand feet tracking one eighty-five, you are entering Iranian airspace," they'd say. Turn right away." Their instruction to "Turn immediately" implied that if we didn't, they'd take action, but they never sent up any aircraft to threaten us. In fact, the only planes that ever threatened us over the Gulf were our own fighter jets, operated by hotshots who thought it would be amusing to annoy us. The longest part of these refuelling flights was the time spent in the air, which may last eight or nine hours. We flew inside our designated "box" in a certain section of the sky throughout this period, listening to sounds from air traffic control, airborne early warning aircraft, and jets heading our way. Every now and again, a fighter or bomber would appear behind us. We'd do our little refuelling dance, and once their tanks were full, they'd resume following and firing on the bad guys. We understood that the planes we fuelled were being used to take down genuine adversaries and protect our men and women, so the work was no different from any other exercise over the United States. This was a critical juncture in the conflict. Between 2003 and 2004, American fatalities nearly doubled and remained at a reasonably high level of around 900 per year for three years. Monthly, the number of wounded approached the same amount. Consider individuals who had life-changing wounds that required amputation or those who suffered from post-traumatic stress disorder to get a sense of how much misery was going on on the ground. When my jet was retrofitted to transport wounded soldiers from nearby Afghanistan to medical care in Germany, I had my closest interaction with combat-wounded soldiers. We could transport more than a dozen soldiers—some in seats, some on guarded gurneys— along with medical personnel, supplies, and devices such as medical-grade oxygen, anaesthetic equipment, and surgery kits. The doctors and nurses were prepared to provide nearly any type of care, including emergency surgeries. Medical evacuation flights were conducted at night, when the enemy would have the most difficulty locating a blacked-out plane flying in an evasive manner. Despite not being fired on, we once had an emergency when the landing gear on one side of the plane failed to retract after takeoff. A dropped wheel and its supports cause drag in flight, which can increase fuel consumption enough to determine whether we reach our goal. We had some luck raising the wheel using a manual crank, but after we had done everything we could, our boom operator glanced out the tiny windows in the belly of the fuselage and noticed that the gear was still hanging. We planned a landing at a midway airstrip, knowing we'd be risking a little fuel. Turkey was the crew's favourite for a silly reason: we knew we could unwind with a drink there. The problem was that the medical team wasn't sure if the Turkish base could provide the high level of care required for one soldier whose serious condition was the primary cause for the travel. This meant either returning to the air base in Bagram, Afghanistan, or taking the danger of an unscheduled, nearly emergency, diversion on the route to Germany. The obvious choice was Bagram. We flew in daylight this time, but there was no anti-aircraft fire. The blocked landing gear disengaged without incident and was repaired by mechanics so that we could depart around fifteen hours later. I walked back halfway through the second flight to see the injured, who ranged from traumatic brain injuries caused by improvised explosive devices to life-threatening wounds sustained in firefights. The first soldier I spoke with, the first newly wounded combatant I had ever spoken with, was in one of the beds. He was virtually bandaged up, and his eyes were full with blood. He could, however, communicate.

"I just want to go back," he explained. "I left my boys behind."

Many people join the military because they love their country, but they fight hard because of the relationships they develop with one another. The tighter the relationship, the greater the risk of their task, until they say they are primarily concerned about the soldiers to their right and left. In general, I viewed American fighters in Afghanistan to be motivated and positive, at least prior to 2010. I believe this was due to the fact that there was no significant controversy around their deployment, as there was in Iraq, and residents, particularly women liberated from harsh religious laws, stated that their lives were better than they had been under the Taliban.

On October 6, 2001, the World Trade Center site was still burning when American bombs and cruise missiles rained down on Afghanistan, where the Taliban government had shielded Al Qaeda. Our first ground soldiers came twelve days later, and we conquered the country in a matter of weeks with the help of our friends. When we traced Osama bin Laden to the foothills of Pakistan in December, he escaped, we were denied complete triumph. Nonetheless, the rapid and strong approach was deemed such a huge success that resources were redirected to Iraq after the country was more or less stabilised. Things had become so bad in Iraq that by 2006, the White House had decided to send around 25,000 more troops—dubbed a "surge"—to try to reverse a rise in coalition losses and restore safety to cities and towns. Millions of Iraqis were terrified to go to work, shop, go to school, or pray at a mosque for fear of being caught in a conflict or being forced to pay a bribe to an insurgent "tax" collector.

One essential to making life safer for ordinary Iraqis and our forces would be to remove (a euphemism for "kill" or "capture") the ground-level commanders who were directing the enemy's hit-and-run operations and receiving supplies and even tactical guidance from Iran's military. (This was the country where people labelled the US "the Great Satan" and marched chanting "Death to America.") New Iranian-made mines that might puncture our armoured vehicles were very alarming to us. The difficulty was that these individuals were difficult to discover, and if they were found thanks to a heroic effort or a lucky break, many of them moved before a team could be created and dispatched to find them. The same could be said for the Iranian advisers, who were difficult to trace as they entered and exited the nation.

According to one tale I heard, this issue arose in a command centre when two generals—one Army, one Air Force—met in a lavatory. The Army general expressed dissatisfaction with opponents who escaped due to insufficient surveillance. The Air Force commander explained that he had a solution: a small surveillance plane flown by the Air National Guard. The RC-26 was a two-engine turboprop aircraft outfitted with electronic eavesdropping gear and video cameras. It could fly quickly and low, intercepting signals from thousands of cell phones. When one matched a number known to be used by insurgents or their Iranian backers, the system was able to determine the position, collect video of the area, and immediately transfer both to ground troops. A target could be reached in minutes rather than hours with the correct coordination. I transferred from the KC-135 wing in Milwaukee to the RC-26 group in Madison, Wisconsin, because I wanted to be more directly involved in the war. After training, I was sent back to the battlefield. But this time I was stationed in Iraq, at a combined Army and Air Force installation in Balad, roughly fifty miles north of Baghdad. Because no one was supposed to know what we were doing—in fact, no one knew we existed—our unmarked facilities were in buildings apart from the rest. We were not allowed to take photos or tell anyone about what we were doing. The fact that the RC-26, a converted Fairchild Metroliner, appears to be the type of plane employed to ferry bigwigs enhanced the secrecy. We pilots joined ground operatives from Task Force 16 and Task Force 17, which were elite troops within the Special Operations structure, at Balad. These were the fighters that would rush to the locations we had pinpointed and either kill or capture the enemy. A third component involved people who may be described as informants. Some kept tabs on rebels in Iraqi cities ranging from Tikrit to Baghdad. Others were CIA spies working in Iran to help us figure out who was talking to whom. This data was used to track phone connections.

The CIA was hesitant to utilise its personnel in Iran to track key individuals in the cross-border plan. The spy chiefs said that the mission was too dangerous, but it's also plausible that they were worried by the prospect of the military carrying out an extensive, indefinite clandestine operation outside of their control. Our side refused to accept no for an answer and continued to push. It took a year, but the CIA finally agreed. The work, frequently referred to as "man hunting," began. The target-kill-or-capture work was difficult, but we had been chosen based on our abilities. Our ground forces were the most ferocious, well-trained, well-equipped, and motivated in the world. And, owing to information from our spies in both Iran and Iraq, including a long-running network run by our Kurdish allies, we received accurate reports on who we should search for and where they may be. This does not imply that the teams performed all of their assignments without difficulty. Critics said that the operators acted too aggressively and violently. Of course, these critics were not present, putting their own lives in danger. A different squad tracked a prominent Iranian figure flying into Baghdad in one of the rare RC-26 operations made public. They were flying over the city when they noticed his cell phone signal coming from an airport terminal and decided to check the taxi wait. The plane's video cameras confirmed his identity when he emerged from the terminal. Our ground troops moved quickly and apprehended him. Sent by Iran's elite Quds Force, whose paranoia over Israel is pervasive, the captive initially mistook our men for Israelis. (So much for the belief that they are the only ones with the most effective commando teams.) Unfortunately, what happened next revealed that we were also up against political impediments that could be more difficult than practical ones. Because of the captive's diplomatic passport and fear of retaliation, the Iraqi government agreed to release him. Local officials also prohibited access to Baghdad's Sadr City district for fear of agitating the numerous inhabitants who supported the insurgents. This had the consequence of offering a safe haven for terrorists seeking to defeat the US and its allies and seize control of the Iraqi government within the Iraqi capital. Ordinary Iraqis grew impatient and began to claim that their lives had been safer and more economically secure during Saddam's reign. People were hired. The utilities were operational. The children attended regular schools. Many people switched sides, supporting the insurgents over the military they had regarded as liberators. Anti-insurgent missions were far riskier than replenishing aircraft. (By the way, once I was assigned to the RC-26 unit, I never returned to the KC-135.) Departing Balad required the most fancy flying I'd accomplish during the battle. If you don't think hostile small arms fire poses a threat to jets, remember that following Russia's recent invasion, a farmer in Ukraine took down a low-flying enemy fighter with a hunting rifle. The key, as you might expect, is to aim in front of the plane and fire enough rounds to increase your chances. That farmer struck gold. I avoided firing by rushing down the runway and skimming along just high enough to clear the air base fence. I'd then climb quickly and at such a steep angle that small-arms fire couldn't reach us (this is known as "standing a plane on its tail"). I wouldn't say it's impossible to strike us with a bullet, but no one would do it on purpose. A bizarrely lucky shot? Perhaps. A well-timed, deliberate round? Never. The only time I felt threatened in Balad was while I was taxiing and the runway was closed due to incoming fire. Someone apparently analysed it and found that moving a plane under these conditions is more dangerous than staying put. It was agonising to sit there waiting for a mortar to land nearby or, God forbid, directly on top of us. Over time, I found solace in the fact that these alerts were frequently false alarms—they could be triggered by something as innocuous as a welder's torch—or that the oncoming rounds were destroyed by our own defences before they could land. The handful that made it made it to a safe location. With each attack, our team made an effort to track down whoever was shooting at us. The opponent, on the other hand, had techniques to avoid capture. They would, for example, freeze mortar barrels and rounds, swiftly position them in the field, and then flee. The round would fall down the barrel, contact the plate that squeezed the firing pin, and take flight as the tube thawed and expanded. Because mortar tubes were so inexpensive, abandoning them meant nothing, and even though they never struck anything important, these attacks forced us to stop what we were doing and take cover. Like everyone else at Balad, I became accustomed to the "incoming" alarms, which rang so frequently that the base was nicknamed Mortaritaville. Despite the fact that I constantly took cover, I wasn't concerned about a hit on our bunker. Everyone on our team seemed unconcerned about the situation, knowing that after a few minutes of chatting nonsense, we'd be back to work. Unfortunately, my carefree attitude caused me to scare my parents the most throughout my deployment. We were on the phone when the "Incoming, incoming!" alarm went off. It was loud enough for them to hear, and I just yelled, "Hey, I gotta go!" I was relaxed about phoning them back because I had no idea how it would sound to them. In fact, days had passed before I did. During that time, they were straining to keep their worry of me being injured or murdered at bay. That is something I would never do again. From my perspective, the surge was successful because, in addition to expanding our fighting force, the Army became considerably more involved in projects that improved the lives of Iraqis. Street patrols and suppression operations such as ours helped to decrease the violence. Repairs to utilities restored power and water supplies. Schools and other community facilities were renovated and modernised. Normalcy returned as residents emerged from their houses to realise the streets were secure.

This strategy was based on the US Army/Marine Corps Counterinsurgency Field Manual, which recommended a hybrid approach that included intense warfare tailored to no-front-lines wars and more benign relations with civilians. General David Petraeus, the author of the field handbook, had spent much of his career researching the Vietnam War, which the US lost because so many of the people we vowed to liberate from communism had concluded that we were actually making their lives worse. They began to back insurgents who carried conflict into ostensibly secure cities and towns.

Petraeus had concluded that insurgencies flourish when communities lose faith in foreigners who promise but fail to deliver stability, as well as when they lose patience with inept and corrupt local officials. This dissatisfaction can breed nationalism and public resistance that no amount of firepower can defeat. Might, regardless of nation, cannot vanquish those who are certain they are correct.

Some commanders in Iraq did not believe Petraeus' policy would work and resisted implementing it. They reflected an unhealed wound that had opened after Vietnam. The American military's experience following our defeat in Vietnam, as well as the Soviet Union's experience following its failed ten-year war in Afghanistan, suggest that these defeats end up dividing the officer corps that fought and confusing decision-makers who either hesitate to take future action or fail to learn from the past. As you may have noticed, even citizens who were present during the war had strong feelings regarding the decision to go to war, how it was carried out, and the politics behind the conflict. (As the conflict came to a close, nearly no one felt ambivalent. Manipulative politicians and deceitful military officials, according to critics, had blood on their hands. Supporters argued that demonstrators had made it impossible for Washington to allow the correct use of force, and that they should be held responsible for the casualties.)

It became clear to me in Iraq that Vietnam still cast a shadow over the US military. Officers who had fought there were divided into two groups. On one side, there were people who felt that Washington had undermined soldiers, but who also believed that the purpose for going to war was questionable and that diplomacy, aid, and investment should have been employed instead. On the other hand, some argued that the initial military operation was appropriate and that the US could have prevailed if our fighters hadn't been shackled by rash policy.

In a paper written shortly after his release from a POW camp in North Vietnam, future US Senator John McCain criticised the US administration for failing to "explain to its people, young and old, some basic facts of its foreign policy." On his side of the debate, there was widespread agreement that the war was lost by the leaders at the very top, rather than the troops who were unprepared for asymmetrical warfare and did not receive a consistent message about the aims they were expected to achieve. Furthermore, Washington's justification for war—to prevent a communist takeover led by China and the Soviet Union—defied the combatants' experience. They recognized that the fight was a civil war rather than a proxy for the worldwide struggle between communism and democracy. How else could the commitment and persistence of forces that began fighting in 1956 be explained? Two hundred thousand military troops would be lost in South Vietnam. North Vietnam estimated that it lost one million people. Countries with populations of approximately 20 million (North Vietnam) and 17 million (South Vietnam) endured these losses.

Senator John Kerry, who would become McCain's US Senate colleague, represented anti-war veterans and civilians. Kerry became an outspoken activist after serving as a patrol boat commander. He discussed how, instead of going to war, we could have made a substantial commitment to "soft power," which would have entailed investing a large quantity on infrastructure and economic opportunity projects that would have improved the lives of the Vietnamese people. Instead, the US had dropped more than three times the quantity of ordnance used by the Allies during WWII on a territory with few industrial objectives and even fewer big military outposts. If this couldn't win a war in a country the size of New Mexico, we'd never have won with a military effort alone.

Kerry, who went far too far in criticising the behaviour of our troops, later backtracked on his remarks. His first position, however, alienated members of the military and those with strong pro-military feelings. This view remained even after Kerry agreed with McCain on the need to impose accountability on civilian leaders and their military supporters. Both men would vote to approve wars in Iraq and Afghanistan, which were critical components of our reaction to 9/11.

Two major decision-makers in the Bush administration have to be classified as Vietnam generation. During the Vietnam War, Defense Secretary Donald Rumsfeld was a member of Congress. He wasn't a well-known hawk at the time. Before his first campaign, he couldn't decide if he was a liberal or a conservative. By 2002, however, he had become an outspoken supporter of the use of military force. Vice President Dick Cheney agreed with him on this point. (In the aftermath of 9/11, Rumsfeld campaigned vehemently for military action against Saddam Hussein.) Cheney and Rumsfeld led the warrior response to the terror attacks, which gratified many Americans, including myself, who were outraged by what happened and demanded action. Cheney and Rumsfeld both felt that America lost in Vietnam due to insufficient firepower and resolve, which resulted in protracted years of warfare, over 50,000 US casualties, and nationwide anti-war riots. This interpretation of the country's terrible experience also implied that a greater force, unrestrained by rules designed to pacify war opponents, would have succeeded. So, when Iraq became our target, the two hawks successfully pushed for a massive invasion force that would overthrow Saddam, defeat all of his forces, and hand over the country to the Iraqis. Most Americans, including nearly every soldier, were unaware that the military officers who led our forces into Iraq and Afghanistan were personally burdened by the Vietnam legacy because they had either served there or were commissioned soon after the war ended. General Tommy Franks, General George Casey, General John Campbell, General Michael Moseley, and Admiral William Fallon were among those who served as officers throughout the war. Furthermore, every general and admiral who led the Joint Chiefs of Staff had served in the Vietnam War from the day of the 9/11 attacks for the next ten years. President Bush had not fought in Vietnam, although he had served in the military as an undeployed fighter pilot during that time. After 9/11, he appeared to be looking for a way to launch a strong attack on the countries that had helped the terrorists while also encouraging the American people to resume their lives as they had before the attacks. Few would feel the cost now that the draft is over, and the US military is an all-volunteer force, and they may be expected to be more patient than Vietnam-era Americans whose sons were drafted into combat. With all of the fighting done by professional soldiers who were rotated between war and recovery periods back home, many Americans had forgotten about the fighting done in their name half a world away.

Whatever your thoughts were on the basis for the Iraq war, it was clear by the time I arrived that our approach was failing. We had fired nearly every supervisor in Iraq's administration, army, and police. Departments were emptied in some circumstances. When local leaders failed to fill the void, our tiny Coalition Provisional Authority demonstrated its inability to govern the country. Crime was on the rise. Utilities remained destroyed, resulting in large numbers of people living without running water and with only irregular power. Some areas still lack safe water today. More than $1 billion in cash had just vanished after being delivered to pay Iraqis who assisted us.

With the situation worsening for everyone save the insurgency, Washington and the allies authorised a so-called surge, which raised the overall force—American and allied—by nearly one-third, and our forces used Petraeus's approach, which he referred to as "clear, hold, and build." Regular soldiers did the clearing, and they then held the region they took. The "build" component entailed creating everything from houses to a free and fair election system from the ground up. Meanwhile, enormous numbers of military police personnel would patrol the streets like civilian police, ensuring long-term safety.

Meeting the soldier with the blood-filled eyes strengthened my resolve to become more intimately involved in the battle. I was motivated more by a desire to protect our men and women than by a desire to murder. After being trained and deployed in the RC-26, I was assigned to the job of defender on our side. It also provided me with qualifications for two aircraft, which is unusual, as well as the opportunity to pilot a plane that is much more exhilarating to fly.

The "more" stemmed from the fact that I was gathering intelligence for Special Operations teams, who would hurry to the site where the equipment packed into the plane identified a mobile phone known to be used by a high-level insurgent. These were the men who either killed our people or planned and directed attacks or IED placement. With each victory, we brought down a local leader.

The surge was effective. In two years, the number of Americans slain fell by around 80%. At the same time, the number of rebels killed increased so dramatically that two years later, the number of enemy fighters we could confront was cut in half. By 2009, our forces were able to walk down numerous Baghdad streets without the full body armour they had previously worn. Infrastructure projects restore power and water services. As shoppers returned, public markets, which sold everything from tomatoes to toilet paper, reverted to being safe, lively places of business. On street corners and in cafés, Iraqis and our soldiers exchanged pleasantries.

In the fall of 2008, General Petraeus was relocated from Iraq to central command in the United States. General Raymond Odierno, who rose through the ranks as an artillery officer rather than a counterinsurgency leader, would take over day-to-day command of the battle. An immediate troop pullback would follow, and we would swiftly return to pre-surge levels.

Back in the United States, a torrent of news reporting and expert studies completely debunked the premise that Saddam possessed an atomic weapons program or stocks of poisonous gas or intercontinental ballistic missiles. The majority of Americans did not trust the rationale for the Iraq war, and they felt the same way about the invasion and occupation of Afghanistan. When speaking at the White House Correspondents' Association dinner, President Bush allegedly put a comedic take on the incident. He displayed photographs of himself examining the Oval Office, claiming, "Those weapons of mass destruction have to be somewhere." I would later learn from a high-ranking Bush administration official that Bush regretted launching the attack on Iraq.

As a lower-level officer, I had no influence on any major decisions taken in Iraq. As a Midwesterner who returned home to see pro-military folks voicing scepticism, the gulf between the people and their leaders prompted me to consider how I could better serve. I did believe that my experience in the military, local government, and as a citizen of Heartland America provided me with a unique perspective. I was also, to be honest, possessed of a large enough ego to believe that I should be involved. As a result, I decided to return home and run for Congress in the 2010 election.

CHAPTER 6
MY CUP OF TEA

Everyone appears to enter politics for the same reasons. They claim to be patriotic. They have solutions to major issues. They believe they have been called by the people, the times, God, or the universe. I identify myself among those who are drawn to politics for the service aspect and to make things better for others, whether it's spiritual or intellectual, or an example provided by family. When I announced my candidacy for Congress on May 19, 2009, in front of an audience of nine people gathered at the Boy Scout Museum in Ottawa, Illinois, I emphasised my desire to win so that I could safeguard our liberties and, wherever possible, make life a little bit better for us all. "There are 700,000 people in this district, and they deserve to see a different kind of Republican candidate," I said, adding that I would reach out to everyone, including Black and Hispanic voters who tend to vote Democratic but share my views. But there is another universal motive for entering politics: ego. Nobody says anything about it, but who raises their hand and says, "Yeah, I think I should help guide the fate of the world's most powerful country"? The only people who do this have either a healthy ego, which represents optimism and self-esteem, or a diseased ego, which indicates hazardous insecurity. Ronald Reagan, a cheerful optimist, with a healthy ego. The malignancy of President Donald "Only I Can Fix It" Trump's ego was apparent at practically every appearance, from his inaugural address, in which he warned of "American carnage," to his petulant last day in office, when he departed without addressing his successor. In retrospect, I realised that I initially campaigned for high office because of my ego, which is similar to Reagan's but not Trump's. I know this because my desire to serve began as a child's idealism, when Reagan was president and made it look cool. I'd been practising for it since I was in elementary school, putting up yard signs for candidates like a big leaguer who starts in Little League. I'd accompanied my father to political events, studied political science in college, ran for and won a county board position at the age of twenty, and then managed my father's state senate campaign.

In 2007, I talked to the press about running against a popular Republican House member in a primary election, only to back down because I didn't think I could win. But it required a lot of guts to accomplish that. It also took guts to have a friend launch a website called draftadam.com before I revealed my intention to run. This strategy worked wonders, garnering press attention and creating the impression that there was a groundswell of more individuals than just the two of us. (Or four, if you count my parents.) However, this was a lighthearted prank that was ultimately meaningless. When I finally announced my candidacy for Congress, there would be four other Republicans and no GOP incumbent to face in a primary since, for the first time since 1995, the position was occupied by a Democrat. Debbie Halvorson, a former state senator, was elected in 2008 on the massive wave that presidential candidate Barack Obama rode: 62 percent of the state vote and an 8.2 percent national victory. She had benefited from the GOP candidate's lacklustre performance as well as a personal profile that would have appealed to people in the district: she had four children and worked seventeen years as a Mary Kay cosmetics saleswoman before entering politics (many mothers in the area sold beauty products to friends and neighbours). She had been the state senate's first female president and had survived a major cancer diagnosis before running for Congress. Naturally, I had my own profile. It encompassed my faith, my previous involvement with the Christian conservative political movement, and my family's farming legacy, which was still going on and tied me to the region's past. Add to that my experience as a combat pilot and my previous duty as a municipal politician, and I have a lot of advantages. Also, as a first-time candidate, I was not encumbered with gaffes, misstatements, or a track record of legislative votes, which is always a benefit for a rookie. I was also moderate enough to declare my support for Obama's decision to send more soldiers to Afghanistan and to gain the backing of local unions, which virtually always supported Democrats. My moderate conservatism was regarded positively, especially in a swing district where voters were eager to support either party. And I believe my similarly moderate demeanour—generally happy, respectful, and open to listen—was also beneficial. I can easily smile and laugh, and if you don't think this counts in politics, think again. People have been demonstrated in experiment after experiment to be very good at determining whether candidates are Democrats or Republicans by glancing at their looks. Democrats are described as warm, affable, and trustworthy, whereas Republicans are described as powerful, domineering, and mature. People accurately differentiate the two groups, giving the impression that they base their votes on what they see in a person's face. But what if you are genuinely kind and trustworthy while simultaneously appearing powerful and mature? Based on the input I received, I came off as having all of these characteristics, which made me a viable candidate in a divided district. Interestingly, and this was something I didn't recognize at the time, my crossover appeal worked in my district but wasn't going to be a long-term benefit in the GOP. I didn't realise how deeply embedded the Republican Party's culture war, which began in the 1990s with passionate and outspoken warnings about the so-called homosexual agenda, cultural diversity, immigration, and liberal sexual mores, had become. This kind of identity politics seemed to me to be anathema to conservatives. We had always objected to the way Democrats seemed to prioritise one group over another rather than pursuing unity. Second, despite growing up in a pretty orthodox faith, I respected everyone's religious journey. I was against abortion, but I didn't think the other side was bad. Finally, I decided to run on the basis of my personal character and policy interests. To put it another way, I would run as a trustworthy, moral man with a positive purpose, not as an angry man determined to stop someone else. Regular, traditional Republicans were still thriving in Illinois' 11th Congressional District, as they were around the country, at the start of 2009. In fact, evidence from the 2008 election showed that our presidential candidate, John McCain, would have benefited from having one of us as his running mate. Instead, he appointed Alaska Governor Sarah Palin, whose involvement with the Christian Right political movement sparked widespread criticism. McCain's problem was that Palin was never going to modify her stances. Palin, who was raised in an intensely political Assembly of God church, wants to link her version of faith with the government and mandate schools to teach the Bible's creation story—how God created the cosmos, earth, and all living things in six days around seven thousand years ago. Supporters of "creationism" claim that dinosaurs coexisted with humans. Polls both before and after the election showed that the more people learned about Palin, the less they liked her. The way she merged faith with political politics was beyond the American tradition for a big portion of the GOP, many independents, and very much everyone who considered themselves live-and-let-live Libertarians. Political analysts calculated that she cost McCain 2.1 million votes and pushed many more independents and moderate Republicans to vote for Obama over their party's nominee in research that would take years to complete. The editorial page of The Economist explained, in an evident allusion to Palin, that "for many conservatives, Mr. Obama embodies qualities that their party has abandoned: pragmatism, competence, and respect for the head rather than the heart."

The Economist was correct about the 2008 election, but I was concerned about patterns unrelated to particular candidates like McCain and Palin. I believed we needed to develop our brand in order to appeal to a broader range of voters, particularly younger voters. The age gap contributed to a demographic issue that nearly no one in the GOP appeared willing to address: the mortality divide. Both parties had known for a decade that Republicans had greater death rates. The disparity expanded to the point where Republican mortality exceeded 800 per 100,000 annually, while Democrats died at a rate of around 720. We were clearly heading in the wrong demographic direction. While the political establishment was deconstructing 2008, I was in Iraq for two months in early 2009. In the air, I targeted the enemy for the commandos, who used precision assaults to capture or kill them. On the ground, I was constantly ducking mortar rounds. And, because I was almost convinced that I would soon announce my candidacy for Congress, I considered the subjects I would emphasise in a campaign. Domestically, my main concerns were similar to those of the majority of the country. The biggest economic crisis since the Great Depression, which began in the financial sector in 2007, has turned into a nightmare. Unemployment was skyrocketing. Mortgage delinquencies followed a similar path. Only three states had more foreclosure filings in 2009 than Illinois. Fortunately, less than 2% of those who feared losing their houses did so, because their low values made repossession a losing proposition. I believed the Democrats had made mistakes in attempting to end the crisis, and I would point them out as I ran. I would reassure people that the Bush-era income-tax cuts, which were set to expire in 2010, would be extended, so that families wouldn't face yet another challenge as a result of the economy's collapse. With so many people hurting, especially small-business owners, now was not the time to increase taxes on them. I also believed that, following the federal bailout of financial institutions, which Bush initiated with $700 billion and Obama increased to $1.1 trillion, more should be done to assist families who lost their homes as a result of the mortgage crisis. This was not the most popular point of view, as many people criticised the borrowers for wanting too much housing for their own good. Out-of-control lenders, on the other hand, didn't care if consumers couldn't repay since they simply bundled these subprime loans and sold them to investors expecting a steady cash flow. I was not opposed to saving banking institutions. They are essential to the functioning of the economy. It was, however, deplorable that nothing was done for those who were being forced onto the streets as a result of bargains they had made with loan demons. The majority of my domestic policy ideas were based on conservative orthodoxy, which has historically served as an essential check on liberal excesses. Like most Republicans, I thought it was time to reform Social Security, but despite the opposition's protestations to the contrary, I didn't want to see it go away. I desired tax breaks for enterprises that increased employment, as well as tax policies that encouraged investment in them. I broke from the dominant GOP agenda by agreeing to raise the gas tax to fund infrastructure projects such as repairing decaying roads and bridges and updating facilities such as airports so that we could compete in a global economy. In addition, I chose a more humane approach to health care, which differed from the plain goal of repealing Obamacare. It was unacceptable to me that so many people had access to health care, which is why I proposed a program to establish high-quality free clinics in neglected neighbourhoods. Yes, this would be a government initiative, but there are times when the government must be used to do things that the private sector cannot. My concerns about domestic issues were genuine, but my true passion was for defence and foreign policy. In Iraq, I had completed a type of national security apprenticeship and realised that we were repeating the mistakes we were supposed to avoid. America began its sixth year in Iraq during my early 2009 deployment. This was longer than the interval between our invasion and evacuation from Vietnam.

The approach that was supposed to keep us out of another quagmire has failed. We were in another quagmire, and the new president, Barack Obama, seems prepared to replicate Nixon's error of emphasising the US intention to depart a half-finished task, which Nixon would refer to as "peace with honour." Obama even stated that the majority of our soldiers would be out by August 2010. Common sense tells you that proclaiming your strong wish to leave is absurd. This knowledge confirms to an opponent who will never defeat us on the battlefield that we have lost our will. This is why the Taliban in Afghanistan coined the phrase "You have the watches." We have plenty of time."

I'm sure some of Obama's military advisers persuaded him that we needed to keep the surge going, follow the new counterinsurgency manual, completely defeat the enemy, and properly stabilise the country. But Obama had opposed the war from the start, seeing Saddam as a harsh dictator who posed no threat to the US and the war as a politically motivated adventure. Defense Secretary Donald Rumsfeld's assurance that the war in Iraq "wouldn't last any longer" than five months, as did his deputy's claim that we could cash in Iraq's own assets, most notably oil, to pay for the war, was ludicrous. As the American people became tired of the war, it was President Obama's time to be swayed by politics. His selection would become the focal point of my military/foreign policy critique of his presidency, and I hoped it would resonate with those who listened to my case and recognized me as a legitimate critic. When the other party wins the presidency, assaults on the president become the focus of the next campaign. It has always been like that. With good reason. Only one president had won House seats in his first midterm election in the previous seventy years: George W. Bush, who gained eight House seats in 2002. This was partly due to the surge of support he earned in the aftermath of 9/11, which boosted every Republican on the ballot. But in 2010, Obama and the Democrats couldn't bank on such bipartisan support. This meant that we had a good chance of winning the House, ending the Democrats' control of both the White House and Congress, and blocking any program we disagreed with. If this all sounds like a game of chess, it is. In reality, it's similar to playing three-dimensional chess. At every level—local, state, and national—both parties utilise every means possible to create districts in which their supporters predominate, contest the tiny number of races in which a race will be truly competitive, and then win the House, Senate, or both. The goal here is not to win a game, but to get the ability to develop your ideas while blocking theirs. It is power with a goal. Individual candidates compete in the same three-tiered game to win a primary contest, if one exists, and then the general election. Knowing I needed to win a primary, which turned out to be a five-way contest, I started working on all three levels at the same time. Leadership support was still important in a political campaign a dozen years ago, and I pursued it at all levels. Locally, I received support from town and city council members, county sheriffs, treasurers, board members, and Republican county leaders. Senators and members of the Illinois House arrived at the state level. It would not have been fair for the Illinois Republican Party to choose one of our five candidates for support, but they did provide me with access to critical mailing lists. I know at least some of my opponents did not have access to these since they did not know how to request them. Many candidates also underestimate the significance of momentum. Since August 18, 2006, when the local newspaper reported that I had subdued a knife-wielding man outside a Milwaukee bar and received a national award for my rapid response, I had been mentioned in passing. While no one can plot an emergency on the street, practically anybody can publish editorial articles in local papers, as I did, and while the draftadam.com ploy was a bit of a stunt, there are various methods to let people know you're thinking about running for office and generate some buzz.

When I was invited to meet with the National Republican Congressional Committee in Washington, I knew I was making progress. I was greeted by NRCC chairman Pete Sessions of Texas, an eight-term congressman, and House minority leader John Boehner of Indiana, a ten-term congressman. Despite their same age and House experience, the two were an unexpected partnership. Boehner was a joyful warrior, willing to compromise in the interests of the country, and he always recognized what should be on the agenda. He learned to interact with others at a young age, having been born into a family of twelve. He began working in the family bar when he was eight years old and learnt to play pool like a hustler. He was friendly, outgoing, noisy, passionate, and profane. He referred to unfavourable legislation as "a crap sandwich." He called Iowa Republican Rep. Steve King a "asshole." When Republicans refused to raise the federal debt limit, he warned them to "get your asses in line." He was a chain smoker who enjoyed a drink after growing up in his family's tavern. Sessions, on the other hand, was a bit of a jerk who looked to be more driven to power for the sake of power. He previously stated that the GOP may go to the Taliban for ideas on how to mount a political insurgency. Unlike the Taliban, he did not have a real policy objective. In fact, when we met, his legislative objectives were blank. He personally supported Steve King's plan to deny citizenship to offspring of noncitizens born in the United States. Sessions, the fourth of four children of a renowned Republican attorney and judge who rose to become the head of the Federal Bureau of Investigation, had strong ties to politics and power. President Clinton sacked his father after he was accused of misusing his position's advantages. Attorney General William Barr, the future ringmaster of Trump administration issues, was the one who signed the report and confirmed the charges. He was aware since he had previously worked as George H. W. Bush's attorney general from 1990 to 1991. These two men's actions, one Democrat and one Republican, would have been enough to put a chip on the shoulder of a future congressman. Our get-together was enjoyable and encouraging because of Boehner's charisma, which improved Sessions' attitude. Both men were heavily involved in the attempt to seize control of the House and Senate and terminate the White House's power to pass legislation, but Boehner was plainly competitive without the need to despise the other side. Of course, he thought Democrats were wrong about most things, but he thought he could work with them. I liked him a lot and was grateful when they stated the NRCC would back me up. Boehner told me, "You're exactly what we're looking for." He meant that the party was looking for younger candidates with the necessary background, charm, and elegance to campaign and win. Soon after the meeting, my campaign received a $5,000 gift from the political action committee operated by Virginia Rep. Eric Cantor, Boehner's deputy. The conservative Weekly Standard dubbed him a "sky's the limit" politician, and he was one of three self-styled Young Guns with leadership ambitions, along with Kevin McCarthy of California and Paul Ryan of Wisconsin. They were seen as anti-establishment at a time when John Boehner was the personification of the establishment. Following Cantor's PAC's gift, a flood of funds came from committees run by other members, including Aaron Schock, a rookie representing Peoria and the first person born in the 1980s to serve in Congress. Donations begat donations, and a sense of inevitability formed around my campaign, as money is the lifeblood of big-time politics and a method for people to judge who may be ahead in a contest. Following that came endorsements, largely from people who contacted begging to be included. We had some stationery printed with our campaign letterhead at the top and a list of persons who have endorsed me running down both sides in tiny font. On this stationery, every Republican in the district received a letter. You can be sure that each recipient looked down the list and recognized and respected names. The five-way primary received around 50,000 votes. I received 32 thousand of them.

With the shift from primaries to general elections, campaigning became much simpler but significantly more heated. The race was one of the few that both national parties, particularly mine, thought could be won. Despite the fact that Debbie Halvorson had ended a fourteen-year Republican control on the seat, no one in politics believed the district had turned blue. With an Illinois senator looking poised to become the first Black president in history, many people, including our 11th Congressional District constituents, wanted to be a part of making this happen. The lingering glow of Obama's triumph had caused one of the country's most regarded experts, Larry Sabato of the University of Virginia, to predict Halvorson's victory in January. Despite his distance from the Midwest, I believe Sabato was a few months behind what had transpired to the general attitude since Obama's election. His extended aid to the finance industry and second auto bailout irritated not just conservatives, but also independents and several Democrats who objected when Bush adopted similar actions and refused to accept assertions that these loans would be repaid. (It would take seven years for the government to confirm a $8 billion profit.) Democrats utilised their majorities in the House and Senate to force Obamacare through, and it became law with the president's signature in March. Then there was an outpouring of energy from opponents who had been mobilising against Obama's entire program since before he entered office. It was known as the Tea Party, and it would change Republican politics in ways that no one could have predicted. The Tea Party was a primarily organic protest movement that got major support and encouragement from the deep-pocketed right-wing establishment and the conservative media. The organic component began in 2009, when a young lady in Seattle known as Liberty Belle organised modest protests against Obama's efforts to bail out the economy and pursue health-care reform. Karl Denninger, a software entrepreneur in Chicago, was equally enraged by the banking organisations that collapsed the economy. The Chicago Mercantile Exchange then applauded TV analyst Rick Santelli as he slammed "losers" who couldn't pay their mortgages. Since the large federal bailout of financial firms had spared many of their jobs, the traders' celebrations seemed a touch off-key. However, the diatribe went viral and played a significant role in the Tea Party's emergence. The rank and file consisted primarily of older people who had long harboured great mistrust of the government. They acquired their news from Rush Limbaugh on radio and the Fox television network. These sources painted a picture of an America under continual threat from an out-of-control government, immigrants, anti-America media, gay rights activists, anti-Christians, and a president who may be concealing his Muslim beliefs and may have been born in Kenya, making him illegitimate. On the outside were self-styled militiamen, 9/11 "truthers" who questioned the events of 9/11, and anti-vaccine campaigners. Some others described Obama's election in blatantly or subtly racist terms. Racism, according to critics of the Tea Party, was a driving force behind it. They also claimed that the involvement of major organisations such as Club for Growth, Citizens for a Sound Economy, and FreedomWorks demonstrated that the movement was being exploited by the establishment. According to Jeff Nesbit, a consultant for these organisations at the time, they had long planned a mass movement inspired by the Boston Tea Party. When George W. Bush was president, the campaign for their comrade Ron Paul called for a "tea party money bomb" to fund hard-right candidates. Following Santelli's outburst in 2009, a political consulting firm formed the Tea Party Express and sent a brightly coloured bus on a national tour, paying to train activists, sponsor events, and run websites. FreedomWorks hosted an all-expenses-paid Tea Party "boot camp" in Washington and dispatched teams of specialists to assist groups across the country. It is critical to underline that the demonstrators' zeal and the movement's growth could not have been completely contrived. This became evident to me when the two Tea Party Express buses arrived at a demonstration in New Lenox, Illinois, and a mob of 6,000 to 8,000 people greeted them. Speakers at the rally advocated for reducing the size of the government and opposing President Obama's health-care plan. They spoke as if an actual tragedy, one of many organised by Democrats, was about to devastate the country. Obama had made things tough for himself by making the erroneous assertion, which he may have believed at the time, that everyone would be allowed to maintain their present doctor under his plan. When this was proven to be false, people began to doubt all of his other claims. Leaked legislative drafts showed that the elderly could be denied some services (this was later eliminated) and included a provision that penalised persons who did not have any type of health insurance. Despite my reservations about their methods and views, I couldn't help but admire the enthusiasm the Tea Party gave to the Republican Party. These folks were fired up to vote, and their primary motivation—the intricacies of Obamacare—was genuine and was not taken into account as the Democrats forced it through. However, as time passed, the movement drifted further and more away from its original concept. Many of the signs held by protesters in New Lenox bore messages that had nothing to do with the original Tea Party agenda, such as false claims that Obama was not a US citizen, calls for more religion in government, complaints about the federal deficit, demands for gun rights, and, in one case, a call for the country to "outlaw GSEs," which are government-sponsored enterprises, such as semi public agencies that backstop mortgages. To attract viewers, Fox News increased its coverage of the Tea Party, sending star pundits Sean Hannity, Neil Cavuto, Greta Van Susteren, and Glen Beck to rallies. Beck's show got the most viewers despite airing in the late afternoon, when many working people were not available to watch. He ascended to this position by literally crying and weeping about the end of America and then championing the Tea Party's ability to save the country. By the summer of 2009, Tea Partiers were squeezing into senators' and House members' town halls, which were generally sleepy information sessions, and shutting them down with their own yelling and screaming. Some sessions became so tense that the member leading the town hall fled for fear of their safety, and police hauled people outside. Senator Arlen Specter of Pennsylvania had to be rescued after protesters began following him around. Scuffles erupted in Florida when demonstrators were unable to join an overcrowded meeting where 1500 people had taken up every available seat. Those who had been barred from entering hammered on the doors so loudly that the speakers could not be heard. Sean Hannity, a Fox News presenter, placed a banner on his website on Friday, July 31 that said, "Become a part of the mob! Attend a Town Hall on Obamacare near you!"

Hannity was one of the trusted sources inside the news bubble occupied by the section of America that would supply the movement's foot soldiers, which had a little more than 10% support from the country as a whole; as little as this may appear, it represented 13 million votes. As polls and more in-depth surveys subsequently revealed, Tea Partiers belonged to the Fox News demographic, which was older, wealthier, and more religiously conservative than their generation and the general population. Worried that they would foot the lion's part of the health-care tab and receive little in return, they were considerably more inclined to believe their situation would deteriorate. They were overwhelmingly opposed to government dollars being used to subsidise schools in minority communities in order to bring them up to par with those in white-majority communities. By the end of 2009, the Tea Party movement had been splintered by lawsuits, strategic conflicts, and an attempt by a national establishment group to link Tea Partiers to a long-term political objective. People at the protests didn't seem to know or care about the higher-level internal battles. The same lack of outrage occurred in 2010 when it was revealed that the Tea Party Express had spent $100,000 on an Alaska cruise for staff members. During my campaign, I made it a point to warn would-be Tea Party thugs, "Let's keep the conversation respectable." This message, which they obeyed, enabled me to accept their assistance while avoiding the worst features of the national movement, which was infamous for disrupting public gatherings and drowning out individuals with opposing views. "Let us begin by respecting one another," I stated in 2009. We can fix the system if we work together civilly. I am determined to look after you."

By April 2010, the Republican establishment had seen surveys that showed me going neck and neck with Halvorson in our race for Congress, and contributions and spending by outside groups had topped $2 million. This was still far short of Halvorson's final tally of $2.5 million, but it meant we could compete. As it became evident that our local Tea Partiers would not use intimidation techniques to disrupt public events, I began using the pronoun "we" to refer to the movement. I also accepted Sarah Palin's support, despite the fact that she never asked if I wanted it. This only strengthened the Tea Party's position. The Associated Press mentioned my campaign in a piece about how it was eating away at Halvorson's lead. But that's when things turned a lot nastier than I could have imagined.

A charge of stolen valour is one of the most heinous things someone can say against a service man or veteran. Hearing whispers about me faking portions of my military service infuriated me, and as evidence grew that one of her subordinates was the source, Halvorson fired him. Then there were others carrying banners calling me a Nazi, which Halvorson denounced, saying her team had nothing to do with it. I trusted her. Finally, there were the campaign advertisements. Halvorson twisted my support for allowing corporations to compete by investing abroad in China into the notion that I was either a double agent or a dupe in a mailer. A photo of me overlaid on a Chinese flag emphasised the message. In a TV commercial, she said condescendingly, "Young man, you have no idea what you are doing." As the former Mary Kay lady ran, interest in the race soared. Our contest had piqued the public's curiosity by the time we began a series of debates. Crowds grew to 500 or more, indicating a strong turnout for a presidential primary contender. She accused me of wanting to gut Social Security when all I sought was to improve its long-term finances. According to her, my preference for keeping the Bush tax cuts to provide certainty to businesses became a handout to the wealthy. Among the more specific local issues I exploited was Halvorson's refusal to hold town hall meetings following the Tea Party storms. There were ways she might have done this securely while still demonstrating her want to hear from the people. Her refusal was a devastating self-inflicted wound.

Throughout the campaign, I countered Halvorson's classic attack with criticisms that highlighted both her background as a politician and her ties to Obama, whom she backed at every opportunity. We also contended that she was a puppet of House Speaker Nancy Pelosi, whom the GOP properly portrayed as a California leftist and member of the coastal elites that many Midwesterners distrusted. I could make these points using boilerplate phrases and snappy retorts that the party thought were on-brand and appealing press bait.

Brand politics explains why, for at least fifty years, the same campaign clichés have proliferated. "We want good things for everyone," said the Democrats. They want to eliminate Social Security and Medicare, take food away from children, free the wealthy from all taxes, and trash the world to oblivion." "We're the responsible realists who will keep you safe and reduce your tax burden," we say. Those individuals despise industry and religion, and they have yet to encounter a government program that does not expand in size every year."

Every Republican congressional candidate was required to talk about how we were superior at handling the economy, preventing crime, generating employment, and defending the country. None of this was fair, but like the Democrats, we were determined to win at whatever cost. And, as I discovered, we had some of the best words to throw at the other side, due to Frank Luntz, a very adept pollster and campaign strategist. He created the list of attack words—corrupt, sad, sick, stupid, traitors—that helped Newt Gingrich gain the Republican House majority in 1994. I wouldn't use the bad ones— well, maybe the milder negatives like crisis and status quo—but I would use the positive ones like duty, freedom, and common sense.

CHAPTER 7
A NEW NORMAL

I believed the Tea Party would die out after 2012. So did the Republican establishment. Despite the purported vitality of the movement, Mitt Romney and Paul—the thinker—Ryan were beaten by Barack Obama and Joe Biden. The GOP's election "autopsy" of this defeat concluded that we needed to recruit more LGBT, Black, Hispanic, Asian, and younger voters. The authors of the paper cautioned that ideological "purity" would lead to disaster. The Tea Party-style absolutists' resistance to all gun control, most environmental safeguards, and all of Obamacare had to be entirely eradicated, or we would never win over a majority of Americans. Fortunately, as the analysis suggested, the purity issue was downplayed in the 2014 midterm elections, and it worked. David Jolly of Florida defeated the Tea Party in both a special election and the general election, winning with 75% of the vote. Other moderate candidates who succeeded with comparable policy ideas were Dan Newhouse in Washington State, Bob Dold in Illinois, Bruce Poliquin in Maine, and Tom MacArthur in New Jersey. The rationale for their success was validated by the neutral Pew Research Center, which claimed in 2010 that 50% of Republicans "agreed" with the Tea Party. In 2014, the "agree" group had dropped to 33%.

My 2014 campaign began with a primary challenge from David Hale, the founder of the Rockford Tea Party. Hale, like the movement's leaders around the country, saw Republicans like myself as part of "the surrender caucus." Hale had been a skilled organiser, and his rallies had become so popular that one newspaper photo from an early occasion showed three elderly Catholic nuns in traditional black habits, grinning cheerfully. One of the sisters was holding an American flag. Another was clutching a Gadsden flag with a rattlesnake on a yellow field and the words "Don't Tread on Me." The flag, which was first used during the Revolutionary War, has become an icon of former Confederate states, with Black Americans generally agreeing it had racial undertones. It was frequent at Tea Party gatherings. Despite the apparent addition of Catholics to the Evangelical/Tea Party cause, as well as the intensity on display at several of Hale's rallies, I won the primary by a three-to-one margin.

The Joliet Herald News stated Kinzinger had defeated his tea party opponent, and polls showed that even the district's Democrats were pleased with me. In the general election, their party's sacrificial lamb hardly ran, and I received more than 70% of the vote. The rising of the moderates signalled that everything had returned to normal. That sounds a little funny now.

Of course, "normal" is a broad term. It can define something objective, such as annual rainfall or planet positions. However, when it comes to humans, normal is relative. Who knows what constitutes a typical diet, weight, or haircut. We may have thought we could answer these questions, but the truth lies somewhere in the middle. In politics, normal might vary depending on your age or the point at which you became interested in a candidate's cause. Normal is a mature style for certain Republicans. It advocates for civil debate, respect for institutions, and opposition to dramatic change. Others, who were growing in number, see it as partisan warfare in an eternal struggle. I became aware of parties, elections, and governance as a precocious child—at least in terms of politics—around the age of six, when Ronald Reagan was reelected to a second term. I could tell my parents adored Reagan because he was always surrounded by the trappings of the office. The presidential seal, Air Force One, and the Secret Service were all impressive. But the president's grandfatherly warmth was more essential. His friendliness calmed critics and gave the impression that everything would be fine. The feelings I felt while watching and listening to the president shaped my idea of someone who could lead all of the people, with emotions always outweighing knowledge. In contrast to my understanding of the administration, I knew little about the Republican Party's congressional agenda and how it was being pushed, and I couldn't name more than a few House members. I wasn't the only one. Most people had no notion that House Republicans were progressively drifting away from Reagan at the time. Even insiders couldn't see where they were going. The quantity of people you would have to track to see a pattern clouded the facts, as did their rhetoric. Members of the House GOP continued to profess their love for Reagan long after they had abandoned his gentler approach and spirit of bipartisan agreement. These words of adulation made it appear as if nothing had changed, when in reality they were masking their wrath at being in the minority and lacking true power.

The House Republicans' poorly veiled rage went against our political heritage, which relied on the decency barriers that permitted Washington to get things done. Since Democrats had dominated the House of Representatives for over fifty years, genuine dissatisfaction made sense. If the Democrats worked together, they could stop whatever we offered. However, because both parties had a sizable proportion of moderate members, concessions were inevitable. Nobody would be completely content with these agreements, which were regarded as the best outcome for everyone, including a citizenry with a diverse set of opinions and interests. What House members and senators referred to as "comity" was gradually fading. House Republicans were frequently blowing through the barriers, which eventually made both sides more confrontational. Reaganism in the Republican Party, as well as Clintonism in the Democratic Party, has waned. Everyone's main goal became power, which could be used to either force a plan through the system or create congestion to keep the opposing side at bay. No one mentioned how the corruption of power that we Republicans observed in the Democrats (power generally breeds corruption) was likely to harm us as well. In its mission statement, William F. Buckley's National Review mirrored the conservative movement's desire to "athwart history, yelling Stop, at a time when no one is inclined to do so." Buckley is the undisputed founder of modern conservative ideology, whose piercing debate style was matched by his respect for others and profound gratitude for his nation. His impact was significant and lasted for three decades, until the movement's rank and file replaced policy and deliberation with ambition. If my early exposure to the Christian Coalition showed me the possibility of a large-scale melding of religion and Republican politics, the Tea Party's use of religious and political symbols demonstrated how the hybrid could be weaponized. In retrospect, it's difficult for me to think that I didn't recognize the scope of what was going on, even in my own congressional district. People approached me in greater numbers at restaurants, petrol stations, and convenience stores to tell me what someone on Fox News had said, to insist that I agree and then get irate if I did not. On rare occasions, people approached me to tell me how much they like what they heard me say on television. I was on Fox News so frequently at the time that people began to recognize me in public areas like airports and restaurants. In a nutshell, I was famous, and as I now know, fame is the seductive poison of politics. It might make you feel liked and required, or it can make you feel energetic and eager. And, as with any narcotic, the more you acquire, the more you crave. The initial hook comes from getting selected, similar to a kid who has been sitting on the bench and is finally sent into a game. It is established as the cosmetics artists make you appear wonderful and brush your clothes. The crew then treats you like a valuable commodity—"Do you want water, sir?" Is the earpiece comfortable?—and then the host attempts to get the best performance from you. You always leave with the words "That was great" echoing in your ears and a strong desire to repeat the experience as soon as possible. You've joined the cool kids' club, and you start looking forward to the next TV appearance, which will provide another opportunity for your coworkers to meet you and say, "I saw you on TV." Excellent work!" Personal attention comes from pals who call you repeatedly, some of whom haven't seen you in a long time. This would make anyone feel like a big shot in an era when attention is a currency that brings prestige, opportunity, and influence.

On Fox, where I knew what was expected of me and could succeed by giving typical GOP boilerplate, it was easy to look like a victor. The party's customary argument strategy consisted of simply flipping the opposing side's position—tax increases for the wealthy were job-killing programs—and then riffing on the major issue. If you were to be confrontational, you might argue the Democrats don't care about unemployed people or the threat of terrorism. If you were feeling relaxed, you could suggest they simply didn't understand how the world works. Sometimes it wasn't Congress that chose the topic of the week; it was Fox News or conservative talk radio broadcasters. For example, I once went on Fox News to complain about Obama renaming Mount McKinley Denali, its native name. "People feel like this president is constantly, like, trying to stick it in our eye," I went on to say. Then I inquired whether it occurred because McKinley was a Republican. Others raised similar concerns. John Kasich, a

Republican presidential candidate, said Obama "overstepped his bounds." Rep. Ralph Ragula referred to him as a "dictator."

My remarks about the name change of a mountain fit into my party's script, which encouraged fast, memorable sound bites and put-downs almost entirely. Typically, the process began with a high-ranking party leader, such as the National Republican Congressional Committee, or someone in the media isolating a sound bite and evaluating how it could be utilised against the Democrats while simultaneously rousing our support. Meetings, phone conversations, emails, and faxes would be used to discuss the talking points. In this example, Obama was aligning the federal government with Alaska, which has been using the Koyukon people's word Denali for forty years. The tribe's name had been in use since before Europeans arrived, and it remained in use until 1898, when a gold prospector renamed it Mount McKinley to help his preferred presidential candidate. We overlooked the underlying rationale and facts that could have benefited the public in our arguments. If they had heard that Obama was attempting to honour Indigenous people, they might have felt better about their country doing something that demonstrated how different we were from forefathers who engaged in everything from thievery to treaty violations to genocidal warfare. We yelled "Political correctness!" instead of being reasonable and admitting there was another side to the story. The scenario escalated from there. The columnist Ben Shapiro, one of the more extreme voices on the right, exploited the recent terrible assassination of a Black youngster named Trayvon Martin by wondering why Obama didn't alter the name to "Mt. Trayvon." According to the far-right website Gateway Pundit, Obama committed a racist gesture since President McKinley was white. Gateway Pundit, like us, jumped on the Denali issue because it worked. Had our constituents swamped the offices of their senators and representatives to express their displeasure with the change? I seriously doubt it. What mattered was that we could rack up points on Fox and, because no Democrats would appear with us, run up the total. I'm not going to lie, I'm having a good time. I did. Whenever possible, the Democrats did the same. In their case, however, it appeared like they were attempting to corner us on subjects of broader interest, whereas we went for explosive culture-war material. They were also less prone to utilise inflammatory language and phrases. We casually referred to them as "San Francisco-style" Democrats, implying that they were gay fanatics. I avoided confrontational approaches because I believed they were unnecessary in the conservative environment and harmed my reputation outside of it. This more moderate demeanour landed me invites to the prominent big network Sunday shows, where both sides were invited to participate in the debate. Democrats fared well overall, because this format demanded more than a couple of catchy talking points. When I was invited, I studied hard and performed admirably. I also felt privileged to be on the same program as fellow conservative Dick Cheney, liberal Supreme Court justice Sonia Sotomayor, and Democratic congressman Keith Ellison of Minnesota, who was a highly brilliant left-wing firebrand. These are the people I met on ABC's This Week on a Sunday in June 2014. They were great people, and the lineup, with Sotomayor and me in the middle and the others on opposing poles, was a more balanced and hence more interesting group. The audience was also of high calibre. The more I participated in meaningful policy talks, the more I hoped we could move away from hyperpartisanship. According to the data, we were on the verge of a tipping point. 8% of Democrats claimed they were "consistently liberal," while 9% of Republicans said they were "consistently conservative." Neither group seriously considered compromising. Worryingly, the proportion of voters who said they had "mixed" political views had dropped to an all-time low of 39 percent. The media ghettos represented by Fox on the right and MSNBC on the left appeared to be pushing individuals into physical isolation. According to 55% of persistent conservatives and 35% of consistent liberals, it is crucial for them to live in communities where "most people share my political views."

When these political polarisation figures were released in 2014, analysts began warning that polarisation had reached its worst point since the Civil War. I treated this with mistrust since evaluations of political division before the 1950s—roughly 180 years of history— were largely anecdotal. It was preferable to ignore the civil war warnings until we had a clearer understanding of what was going on and could place it in a more historical context. It's likely that I ignored the grim warning of civic unrest because the Air Force had taught me to remain calm even if I was driving a burning tanker. It's also possible that this was something that came naturally to me. My mother, as a teacher, was so calm that her students didn't even consider raising a commotion. My father could work with anyone, from irate program participants to state officials, without becoming agitated. With the exception of a few incidents involving excessive amounts of alcohol, I had always been the type of person who rarely got too high or too low. By middle school, I felt comfortable speaking in front of a crowd, chatting on the radio, or having my ideas published in the local paper. Nothing appeared to disturb me. Civil war also seemed far-fetched because I believed that most of the people who seemed so enraged—on the right and on the left—knew in their hearts that the concerns they were supposed to believe were life and death for themselves and the country were not. Whether they were agitated by ultraliberal broadcaster Keith Olbermann or an entire network in Fox News, they must have realised that these sources were a type of entertainment, designed to elicit emotion, rather than genuine news broadcasts. Even the celebrities said they were not journalists. Rush Limbaugh, a radio comedy genius who kept listeners engaged with conspiracy theories and cliffhangers, was a favourite of my constituents. He even claimed to be an entertainer. Sean Hannity, their second favourite, deemed himself a talk-show host who should not be subjected to the same standards as news reporters. If the Fox News slogan "Fair and Balanced" was a joke, it would be even funnier if applied to Sean.

Although I honestly assumed that everyone was in on Sean and Rush's plan and that their supporters were not as furious as they appeared, I was mistaken. Again. In fact, Fox News was taking over viewers' minds and keeping a majority of individuals in my party hooked on progressively potent items, much like a drug dealer. One notable example was the network's emphasis on the fabricated debate over Obama's birthplace. The hosts insisted that Obama was an illegitimate president who needed to prove he was a "natural-born" American. They feared he was born in Kenya, which, according to the Constitution, would exclude him from the presidency. Obama did, in fact, make his Hawaiian birth certificate public in 2011. Furthermore, the Supreme Court ruled that if your mother or father is an American, you are a "natural-born" US citizen regardless of where you are born. The case is closed.

As I sought to persuade my district's "birthers" of the reality, I learned that mere conversation nearly never worked. Constituents who had doubts about Obama's birthplace occasionally shifted to another theory: Obama had renounced his citizenship when he became an Indonesian citizen as a toddler. There! See?

Obama lived in Indonesia from the age of six to nine, but there is no indication that he became an Indonesian citizen. Indeed, the only way he could have lost his American citizenship would have been to renounce it legally. Children are unable to do so without a consular investigation. There would be some public record if he had done so. And don't you think someone would have discovered it?

Other outlandish Fox assertions that were published as reality included broadcaster Glenn Beck's conspiracy theory concerning Agenda 21, a United Nations document. The paperwork is genuine. It urges action to combat climate change in order to protect the twenty-first century. More than 175 countries signed it, including the United States under Republican President George H. W. Bush. It is nonbinding and confers no jurisdiction on the UN in any country. Nonetheless, Beck swung a few hundred printed sheets about, claiming it was a copy of Agenda 21, and claiming it revealed the UN's goal for world dominance. Beck's claim, when repeated, tapped into a long-standing mistrust of the United Nations among radical conservatives. The John Birch Society has been preaching about the UN's threat to national sovereignty for decades. As a young person, I was exposed to these beliefs. The Birchers were so far-left that they suspected Dwight Eisenhower of being a communist. In the 1960s, this kind of position drove them into oblivion. However, their beliefs reappeared in the 1990s, and a rising proportion of Republicans thought that communists and socialists were taking over the country. In the 2000s, militia organisations circulated the myth that UN detention camps were being set up to support a takeover of the United States, and that flights of so-called black helicopters were proof that they were looking for locations. Helen Chenoweth, a Republican representative from Idaho, stated in 1996 that "we have some proof" of the chopper idea. She never produced it, but the assertion was popular among the paranoiacs. In 2013, many Americans were alarmed after hearing online that helicopters were flying over prospective invasion areas. GOP adviser Dick Morris, ostensibly a serious man, produced a book titled Here Come the Black Helicopters! in 2014. During this time, John Boehner was labelling Fox News host Sean Hannity "a nut" and claiming that Americans were being "brainwashed" by constant assertions about Obama. However, as one of just fifty-one people to hold this high position—third in line to the presidency—Boehner wielded significantly less public clout than Hannity and his colleagues. Their predictions and distortions played in homes, pubs, barbershops, cafés, restaurants, and even some businesses on an eternal loop. The terror and indignation emanating from televisions and radios raises adrenaline levels in listeners, providing an energy boost when the ancient fight-or-flight instinct is awakened. Over time, the condition known as an "adrenaline bath" can lead to obsessive thoughts—for example, about political danger—and a desire for more of the excitement hormone.

Ratings showed that millions upon millions of people were watching the doom shows, but the depth of their impact was shown in one-on-one interactions. After writing a newspaper column against nuclear power with my colleague Cheri Bustos in early 2015, you'd think I'd insulted half the folks in the district. People began to question how I had the audacity to cooperate with Bustos, a Democrat from our state, on anything. It didn't matter that we were pushing a traditional Republican agenda to ensure that nuclear power would continue to be a viable energy source in the future. Then there was the outrage over how the essay I contributed to acknowledge the tiny victories of Obama's attempts to cut unemployment, assist manufacturers in recovering from the Great Recession, and promote exports. He also bucked his party by advocating for more gas and oil output. I also agreed that it was critical that nuclear power would not generate greenhouse gases and that the damage caused by excess carbon would cost up to $18 billion to repair.

I still disagreed with Obama on many issues, from health care to foreign policy, as evidenced by the massive humanitarian calamity in Syria, but you can't talk about the future rationally or constructively if you don't see the present clearly. Fox claimed that climate change research was "fabricated," hence my goal in lowering carbon emissions was misguided. According to Fox, eight million fewer Americans were working in 2009, and the US would need to spend "eight billion dollars a day" on oil that could be pulled out of deposits in the Gulf of Mexico. These were outrageous assertions, but they came from people my constituents trusted more than I did.

The erosion of faith in leaders, authorities, and institutions was and continues to be a major issue. With the exception of a brief rise in the late Clinton/early Bush years, trust in government has been steadily declining for decades. Activists attempted to undermine trust in science, health, education, and other disciplines, aided by those who want to be the sole source of knowledge for as many people as possible. Their efforts were successful, as many individuals began to believe that all experts were questionable and that determining the truth was difficult. They had no idea that those pushing them toward cynicism included tobacco lobbyists who ridiculed medical researchers and fossil fuel operatives who opposed climate science. Our party capitalised on the political energy generated by these activists as people came to dislike specialists.

People's distrust pushed them to conduct their own "research" on websites like Facebook, which makes money by reinforcing users' views. Picking and choosing sources could lead them to someone like Republican operative Andrea Tantaros, who claimed that before the American Revolutionary War, "some guy in Boston got his head blown off because he tried to secretly raise the tax on tea."

Democrats had their own issue with twisting or deleting facts and making false accusations against Republicans. President Obama falsely claimed during his 2012 campaign against Mitt Romney that his opponent was unconcerned about the poor and middle class. During the same year, Obama used some doozies during his final debate with Romney, falsely accusing him of, among other things, wanting Pakistan to control our anti-terrorism efforts and charging, falsely, that Romney would have done nothing to help the auto industry recover from the recent financial crisis.

Although the Democrats' misdeeds were true, they were not as many or outrageous as those on my side, and I sometimes felt that I was dealing with individuals who, in the words of Mark Twain, "refused to let the truth get in the way of a good story." This is why I avoided several of the talking points memos. More significantly, whatever injustice the Democrats inflicted had little impact on people in my district. My people were motivated by the intramural battle for GOP leadership, which demanded constant attention in order to pick out the weaklings, the faithless, and the deceivers. Even as the Tea Party organisations faded into obscurity, the concerns raised by the movement and the complaints they brought to politics remained, and more people appeared to be driven by them. Indeed, the tricorn hats would be quickly replaced with red baseball caps emblazoned with Trump's campaign slogan "Make America Great Again," signalling their support for Donald Trump's 2016 presidential campaign, and there would be considerably more of them.

CHAPTER 8

CARNAGE

Donald Trump stated that 1.5 million people attended his inauguration event. Please give me a break. I sat about five rows up, with a full view of the crowd, for the ceremony, which took place on the West Front of the Capitol. It took up roughly three grids of the National Mall in front of the reflecting pool. It appeared far less than the 1 million I saw gathering at Obama's second inauguration; his first had drawn a record 1.8 million people. Trump's assertion was ridiculous, but it wasn't the most unpleasant aspect of the inauguration weekend. That distinction went to his theatrical behaviour during the swearing-in ceremony, when he took part in the 220-year-old, peaceful-transfer-of-power ceremony that shows our democracy in action to the world and places the burden of the presidency on a person who cannot feel its weight until the oath is spoken. Trump appeared less like a true leader and more like an actor playing in the opening scene of a big-budget film dubbed The President. The arrival of the VIPs, who took their places to the strains of hymns and marches played by the Marine Band, kicked off this section of the ceremony. Members of Congress, Supreme Court justices, outgoing President Barack Obama, and former Presidents Jimmy Carter, George W. Bush, and Bill Clinton were among them. It was a parade of power and history. The music came to a halt just as a presenter with a loud baritone voice announced the arrival of Vice President-elect Mike Pence and those in charge of organising the event. Then he remarked, "Ladies and gentlemen, the president-elect of the United States, Donald John Trump."

Marines in their dress uniforms—blue coats, white belts, and caps—opened and held the two brass doors at the top of the stairs. Donald Trump emerged from behind the canopy about fifteen feet from the door, his overcoat and suit jacket unzipped to reveal his white shirt and distinctive extra-long necktie. It's likely that no president-elect has ever dressed so casually. Later, I checked, and everyone who had been photographed had buttoned up. Those in the crowd who missed this display of swagger were most likely captivated by the red tie that cascaded over his belly and fell six inches below his waist. It was like a red arrow sign at a car wash, pointing attention to his genitals rather than the line of automobiles waiting to be cleaned. Nothing in his appearance—not his dyed golden hair, nor the orangey skin, nor the tie—was inadvertent for a guy wonderfully attuned to image and stagecraft. Everyone else's ties were always longer than his. Even when the colour wasn't red. Trump came to a halt at the top of the stairs and raised a single fist, resembling so many autocrats depicted in history books. He then walked down the carpeted stairwell slowly, enjoying every tick of the thirty seconds it took to descend twelve stairs and walk the same number of steps to reach the front row. Melania, his unsmiling wife, gave him a no-contact air kiss there. He greeted the Obamas and Vice President Biden before taking his seat in the centre of the stage. Thirty minutes went by as the congregation heard several invocations and prayers. The University of Missouri Chorale, the Mormon Tabernacle Choir, and the Marine Band provided music. Trump took the oath of office, promising to respect the Constitution, and then stepped in front of a podium bearing the presidential seal for the first time. Whereas Kennedy asked Americans to consider what they might do for their country and Reagan pledged that we could protect "this last great bastion of freedom," Trump presented a dismal America. The phrase "American carnage" would become synonymous with the speech almost immediately. Trump boasted of his election by a movement "the likes of which the world has never seen" in a speech that was mercifully brief, and contrasted this with a landscape he dubbed "American carnage" in the form of lost jobs, dropping salaries, and poverty. His personal theme—the unequalled quality of his support—was an unbecoming brag that was belied by reality. Forget about the world. Trump's public support was nowhere near that of LBJ, Reagan, or even William Henry Harrison, who were all elected by groundswells. Set aside, if you must, the fact that he was defeated in the popular vote by over two million votes. His Electoral College victory margin was so narrow that it placed 48th out of 56 in history. Trump's other theme, economic "carnage," drew on conditions caused by the Great Recession, which began in 2007, and ignored seventy-five straight months of job growth, a GDP rising faster than it had in five decades, and a 5.4 percent increase in household income the previous year. In addition, the poverty rate had fallen for two years in a row and was now close to the previous fifty-year median of 12.5 percent. Trump had demonstrated his preference for stagecraft over honesty and fantasy over truth by concluding with unenthusiastic shout-outs to faith and unity. "God bless America," he said as he jutted out his chin, frowned his forehead, and raised another fist. He raised it higher than previously and shook it at the audience. Trump came to a halt as he approached his chair, turning around to face the crowd after shaking hands with adjacent dignitaries. He knew how to seize the occasion as a seasoned stage performer. He hopped back onto the platform that raised the podium and pumped his hands in the air. The same as Rocky Balboa. The crowd's applause became a little louder. I cheered grudgingly, as did Senate Majority Leader Mitch McConnell and House Speaker Paul Ryan. For emphasis, Trump and Obama shook hands and grabbed each other's left arm. They exchanged a few words, with Obama stating, "Good job." As he reached her, First Lady Melania Trump, who had only smiled when her husband looked at her directly, kept a hard demeanour and offered him simply a nod and two or three words. It would appear that the new First Lady foresaw what was to come. The two things I remember most from the 2017 Republican legislative planning conference in Philadelphia were that Donald Trump spoke and acted just like the person you saw on TV during the campaign, and that I got... hmmm, what's that term... oh yes, shit-faced. In fact, I became the most inebriated I had ever been. And I'm only now beginning to realise why.

First and foremost, the sight and sound of Donald Trump giving a speech in person, which I had avoided up until this point, shook me. During the campaign, he stated, "I can be more presidential than anybody." He may have chosen to depict himself as president, assuaging our worries. Instead, he opted to speak in the manner of the man who stated, "I could stand in the middle of Fifth Avenue and shoot somebody and not lose any voters." He reiterated absurd claims, such as Mexico paying for his border wall, and declared as fact that "Democrats are determined to replicate the most catastrophic failures of world history right here in the United States."

"Is this really our president?" I wondered as I listened. I knew we'd had some awful choices, but this guy was worse than Franklin Pierce. Trump's main strength was acting like a demonic cheerleader, motivating people to his cause. This shadow charisma, on the other hand, was a superpower that formed a hold on the susceptible. After his nomination, and especially after his election, magic has worked on both the Republican Party—my party—and individuals. Nothing he could do or say would be able to break the bond. It's difficult to give credit to Trump's nonsense. He began with some elementary-school-level remarks about Philadelphia as the birthplace of American independence. Following that was a jumble of campaign themes, boasting about executive orders, and abrupt non sequiturs. "Paul Ryan and other leaders in Congress and I, and Mike Pence— how good a choice was Vice President Mike Pence?" he said at one point. Then, as if a Vegas act pointing to a celebrity in the audience, Trump waved his arm toward Pence and said, "Stand up." To a sprinkling of applause, Pence did as he was ordered, in a foreshadowing of the many subservient Pence moments to come. "Everybody loves him," Trump stated.

Repealing Obamacare was one of the few policy priorities listed by the incoming president, and here, too, he deviated from the norm. For the past five years, Republicans have promised to repeal the health-care program. He wanted to be the one to fulfil the commitment because he had claimed throughout the campaign, "We'll have so much winning you'll get tired of winning." However, he seemed to realise that his support for this problem was shaky, so he proposed that we do nothing for two years because the program's premiums would climb so high that it would collapse on its own. That's what I mean by hedging your bets. Tom McClintock of California highlighted the misgivings felt by many Republicans in a later health-care policy conversation that we held among ourselves. "We had better be sure that we are prepared to live with the market being created," he went on to say, as "that's going to be called Trumpcare." To emphasise his argument, he said, "Republicans will own it, lock, stock, and barrel, and we'll be judged on that."

McClintock's comment was secretly taped and then made public. This tactic, which provided the leaker with some credibility with a journalist, was characteristic of modern politics. Today, you have to presume that members of the House routinely videotape ostensibly private sessions and, if they think they come across well, share them with the press. No one said anything critical of Donald Trump at the retreat, and no one mentioned that no hint of a better and cheaper alternative to Obamacare had been developed in the twenty months since campaigning Trump first promised it. He fared better with his projected $1 trillion infrastructure plan, but he would never campaign for it to become law. Infrastructure, like his ostensibly fantastic health-care plan, would perpetually be in the yapping stage. During seven so-called infrastructure weeks—remember him getting behind the wheel of a semi truck and pretending to drive?—the babble would mount. That never resulted in anything concrete. Of course, at the start of every administration, the party in power envisions not meaningless fighting and false starts, but a string of accomplishments justified by the ostensible mandate supplied by the voters. However, with presidents elected on the smallest of popular vote margins—and occasionally, as in Trump's case, with minority support—the concept of a mandate is a bit of a stretch. Fortunately for us, the GOP kept control of the lower chamber following the 2016 election. A similar outcome occurred in the Senate, when we lost two seats but maintained our majority. This meant that the good men—both parties consider themselves to be the good guys—would have to move quickly and unite before the people gave the evil guys a legislative majority in 2018.

Meanwhile, Republicans in Congress and across the country rallied behind Trump and gave him overwhelming support. One may have hoped that this action represented what author James Surowiecki argues in his book The Wisdom of Crowds, that the public does a good job of making judgments and picking a direction based on big crowd decisions. Indeed, he claims that crowds are often wiser than individual decision-makers because they take into account the experience and judgement of many minds operating at the same time. It's similar to when scientists use a massive network of personal computers to solve large issues. The wisdom of crowds may explain why people naturally switch between parties, giving one the legislative branch and the other the executive. Something within them desires to limit the extent to which one party can influence events. The people have voiced the concept of checks and balances, which is incorporated in the Constitution. Unfortunately, institutions like the Electoral College can stifle the wisdom of the multitude, which may explain why only one other modern country, Ireland, adopts this system and, like us, recognizes that the chief executive may be chosen by a minority. This reality allows for the reelection of the same president, which explains in part a feature of the retreat that was even more frightening than Trump: my colleagues' nearly universal commitment to his political cult. Members I respected and who I knew thought Trump was a mean-spirited idiot made it apparent that they supported him wholeheartedly. Unsurprisingly, the Freedom Caucus led the charge, reacting to Trump in the same way that Taylor Swift superfans would react to her presence. This rush, however, included practically all of my friends. Billy Long of Missouri, who was in my 2010 class, is a wonderful example. He had focused on regulating and reducing diesel emissions, improving rural broadband access, and funding suicide prevention initiatives. These ideals did not represent Trump's priorities, and Billy abandoned them once it became evident that Trump would use his position ruthlessly to punish disloyal Republicans. Consider how he humiliated senator, former governor, and former Republican presidential nominee Mitt Romney by dangling the secretary of state job at a much-photographed "private" dinner and then selecting ExxonMobil CEO Rex Tillerson. Tillerson's credentials began and ended with his standing as Vladimir Putin's closest American ally. Only four years ago, he signed a $3.2 billion deal to explore for oil in Russia's Arctic. Putin soon after gave him the Russian Medal of Friendship.

Trump anticipated that Tillerson would prioritise US-Russia relations. This proved that what the president dismissively referred to as "this Russia thing" was, in reality, a significant problem. It also prompted me to push for a national initiative to combat Russian disinformation, which was endangering our democracy. Troll farms and the Russian government's Internet Research Agency, which had pounded US social media with disinformation to aid Trump and harm Clinton, were among the precise targets I thought we needed to attack. When it came to Russia, just a few Republicans in Congress were as open to it as I was. This did not imply that I had given up hope for the near future. Only a few adults survived at the top of the administration. The courts may possibly place some constraints on Trump, and despite Trump's aggressive campaign to portray the press as a "enemy of the American people," the press could theoretically probe and broadcast the inevitable scandals that would arise from within the administration. As I adjusted my outlook for the future, I had to account for the very real potential that the slow-moving court system would do little to moderate Trump, as well as the certainty that the administration would have no congressional supervision under GOP control. What about the media? The country had long been divided between conservative and liberal media outlets, leaving few in the middle to receive reality-based reporting. This was not the Watergate era, when every major news organisation worked to limit prejudice and offer accurate information. It was the Fox News/MSNBC era, which meant that over half of the population would be denied the complete truth on any significant subject. A shattered press. A Congress hostage. A legal system that is meant to progress in little steps. No wonder I left the retreat crowd, found a place to drink, and kept going till I could hardly get to my room. The alcohol prescription for my spiritual suffering helped at the time, but the bodily ache I felt when I woke up was not worth it. It became worse when I rolled over, checked the time, and learned I had a CNN crew meeting me in five minutes. I had already learned how to wash, change clothing, and take off at a sprint regardless of how I felt. I went through the motions and arrived at the TV team in time to put on an earpiece and complete a mic check with the control room in New York. The field producer then indicated that there will be a delay.

"You're on camera and the control room can see you're really sweaty," she went on to say. "We're going to hold you for fifteen or twenty minutes so you can cool off."

Although I can't remember what I said in the interview, I evidently played it safe because no one at the retreat mentioned it to me afterwards. And no one mentioned anything about my bloodshot eyes or the little pauses I needed to take when a question was asked. Of course, this may be because the majority of them were either in the same condition I was the night before, or they had been there and done that and would never criticise me for looking a touch green around the gills on TV. Everyone in the national politics business understood that the Washington inhabited by members of Congress—particularly younger members of Congress—was about as drink-soaked as a college fraternity, except that the majority of the wine is free and it usually comes with the best food in town. Consider Animal House, but with costly whiskey instead of beer, matured steaks instead of pizza, and no money needed. Some who partake are social drinkers who know their limits. Others are alcoholics with an extremely high tolerance. If you have any doubts about my reference to addiction, look at the 24-hour schedule for Alcoholics Anonymous meetings in the capital. However, addiction and pleasure drinking do not explain why so many members of Congress, particularly the younger ones, consume so much alcohol. Their insecurity is the true reason. Despite popular belief, many candidates for public service are not natural glad-handing extroverts. Instead, they are continually uneasy introverts attempting to prove something to themselves or others. They were the kids in high school who were rejected by the popular circle but joined the debate team so they could at least vocally defend themselves. Many feel that their election will help them overcome their uncertainty, only to realise that there are popular students in the House as well, and they are difficult to impress. The Freedom Caucus was full of these awkward but envious folks who eventually reverted to type, anxious to be liked. And it was evident. There's also the matter of money. Those who come to Congress with no independent money find it difficult to turn down goodies. This is why fancy DC eateries are frequently jammed with small parties of members in the company of lobbyists who are happy to fatten people with House votes. I use the phrase fatten intentionally because, like college students, members of Congress generally gain a "freshman twenty" pounds as a result of these meals and booze. I did, and it took a year of hard work to get rid of them. One additional advantage: the gym is a perfect place to gather and converse with coworkers without worry of being recorded because you are on the phone. Who can conceal a taping device in a towel wrapped around their waist? Working out allowed me to continue dining high on the menu multiple evenings a week at the cost of interacting with someone who wanted to influence me. However, because my goals and their interests were frequently aligned, and lobbyists are employed for their charming personalities, this sum does not appear to be excessive. Office perks can extend beyond Washington to include overseas travels for official and unofficial business, which turn into opportunities to have fun. But, of course, when you pack dozens of "baby congressmen" on aircraft and buses, unexpected things happen. I went on a fact-finding tour of Israel during my freshman summer. The majority of our daytime excursions were with government officials who showed us defence sites, locations where security is a challenge, and evidence of the country's richness and prosperity as well as its vulnerabilities. As a functioning democracy, Israel is surrounded by potential and actual enemies. It requires American assistance. Since its inception, the country has received more funds from America than any other country. It now flows at a rate of $150 billion each year. This is certainly the most compelling argument for Israelis to serve as delighted hosts to an endless stream of American fact-finders. It is not a question of tolerating us. They seek to improve the US-Israeli relationship by impressing us with firsthand experiences. When you consider how many members of Congress return from these visits as staunch supporters of Israel, you realise that this type of tourism for the powerful works quite well. However, I was already a strong supporter of Israel prior to the trip. We were invited to a celebration on the shores of the Sea of Galilee on the last night of our journey to Israel. Of course, it was free, and our hosts even dispatched a barge to anchor offshore and serve as a platform for technicians to unleash spectacular pyrotechnics. The name of our destination, like so many other places in Israel—Jerusalem, Hebron, Bethlehem—evoked in me and others the religious component of our own identities. The Sea of Galilee is the lake where John the Baptist baptised Jesus. It's where, according to Scripture, he walked on water and fed a swarm of people with a meagre supply of bread and fish that never ran out. Following a supper that began with several shots and featured exquisite wines and after-dinner beverages, we carried out an earlier plan for a swim, with one alteration dictated by the liquor. Because the sea meant so much to so many of us, we decided to mark the occasion by diving in. Instead of wading in properly, the booze convinced us that we could jump in our underwear. I ignored my lousy swimming ability and got thirty feet from shore before panicking. My nervousness drove me to puke in the water (how classy!) and I yelled for aid. I can't remember who helped me, but someone did. When we arrived at the beach, I noticed the guys on the security detail had removed their ties and coats so they could jump in if needed. Fortunately, the situation did not deteriorate to that extent. The next morning, some of my coworkers expressed concern that our swim would be made public. The talk of scandal started. We can see the headline: Congressmen strip and swim in the sacred sea. Because of our mutual fear, no one mentioned the incident until months later, when an item emerged in Politico. The news got out because Republican Dave Schweikert, who was running against Ben Quayle in a primary, was on the Israel trip and leaked it. Following Galilee, I decided to attend only parties where I could talk to people about my district's concerns and the hosts could help us. If I travelled abroad, I would focus on business. Stay away from the water. And I wouldn't allow myself to drink excessively. I performed the same thing in my daily life at home. I dedicated myself to being an excellent Team Player once I stopped being a party-hard companion for other freshmen. Team Players are members who form independent political action committees, generate large sums of money, and then give the funds to other members facing tougher elections. Good Team Player status also necessitates expressing support for everyone in the party while suppressing critical ideas. As a result, I fulfilled what Ronald Reagan referred to as "the eleventh commandment" for good Republicans. Democrats have their own loyalty rules, which explains why Bill Clinton was impeached but not convicted on perjury and obstruction of justice charges stemming from a sexual relationship with a White House intern. Prior to Clinton's impeachment, Republicans stood by Richard Nixon as the Watergate crisis escalated to the point where he resigned from office to avoid the embarrassment and save the country from the political anguish of impeachment. Trump believes Nixon should have remained in office, even if it resulted in a national political catastrophe worse than Watergate. Trump avoided being challenged for several years, much like Nixon. The Trump administration's scandals at the time mostly included small financial corruption of cabinet officials. Despite the unprecedented amount of these financial and ethical scandals—seven in the first year alone—none of them made a big impression on the public. This was due, in part, to Trump's chaotic governance and political practice, which made it difficult for people to keep up, let alone appreciate the significance of any single event. Whether he was tweeting lies, threatening the North Atlantic Treaty Organization, or continuing to deny the Russia affair, Trump had the entire country focused on his strange or unsettling conduct and wondering what would happen next. Although this was somewhat due to his personality, I believe it was also a purposeful plan. Trump adviser Steve Bannon once described the tactic as "flood the zone" in football terms. In football, this is concentrating so many offensive players in one area of the field—a zone—that defenders are unable to keep track of them. The zone for Trump was the amount of time and energy people could dedicate to keeping watch on him. He saturated the "zone" with lies, distractions, and absurdities so anyone attempting to defend themselves would fail. Looking back, it's amazing how many people and institutions Trump denigrated. I was shocked early in his presidency by his attacks on major alliances such as NATO. No institution has been more important to maintaining peace than NATO, and since Trump was supported in the 2016 election by Russian spies, there was no way to dismiss the notion that his campaign to hurt NATO was a thank-you to Putin for all his assistance. This notion gained popularity after Trump returned from a meeting with Putin, claiming that Putin had denied election meddling and that he had no reason to doubt his word. The concept that Trump and the Russians had a political connection was something my party battled with the same zeal that our forefathers fought communism and the expansionist aims of the other Soviet Union. Members of my party saw that the present dictatorship in Moscow, led by a former Soviet spy named Vladimir Putin, was just as eager for empire as the old USSR, as seen by an unjustified invasion and occupation of sections of Ukraine. They were also aware that one of Trump's campaign advisers had communicated with Russian authorities about receiving assistance, and that the campaign had a manager who had served as a political operative in Moscow and Ukraine and owed about $20 million to one of Putin's oligarch friends. This came after the Republican National Convention reneged on its long-standing pledge to help Ukraine against Russian aggression. As my Republican colleagues in Congress rallied behind Trump on the Russia issue, I stood firm in my support for Ukrainian independence and security. As Trump sent out thousands of social media messages to his seventy million followers, who replied by assaulting other politicians, including Republicans, the tone in the caucus became paranoid. Any discussion of Trump's shortcomings—the man was actually unsuited for office—occurred in private between individuals who had made it clear they shared the same viewpoint. It astounded me to witness how apparently adult members of Congress quiver at the prospect of being attacked by a tweet or Facebook post. It reminded me of the first Twilight Zone episode "It's a Good Life."

The plot concentrated around Anthony, a monster mind-reading youngster with the ability to destroy everything with a single thought. Set in the last remaining society on Earth, it depicts the painstaking efforts adults make to prevent even thinking of anything bad. It concludes with Anthony still in charge, ordering the adults to do whatever he wants. Fearing Trump's capacity to derail their careers, twenty-six House Republicans, the most since 1972, resigned before running for reelection in 2018. This spared them the humiliation of losing to a Trump-backed primary challenger and relieved them of the stress of living in a place where the safe topics of conversation were baseball, the weather, and Trump's successes, which included tax cuts, judicial appointments, and smaller measures such as the establishment of a medical-care hotline for military veterans. On the Senate side of the Capitol, two Trump critics whose mandates were coming to an end, Tennessee's Bob Corker and Arizona's Jeff Flake, resigned rather than face challenging primaries. In his parting remarks on the Senate floor, Flake expressed his own unhappiness with paralysis and an angry politics, as well as his concern about Trump. "There are times when we must risk our careers in favour of our principles," he went on to say. "Now is such a time." He expressed concern over the Senate's "complicity" with the unacceptable. "I rise to say, enough." Flake's reelection was doubtful, as Trump's allies pointed out as they mocked him as a traitor. Others said that he should have fought the fight in the hope of winning and then returned to Congress to do all they could to either contradict or lead the president. The latter presumed he desired to be directed toward more rational action. Speaker Ryan and Senate Majority Leader McConnell attempted to instruct Trump on how to rule, which is impossible to do by creating fights, rejecting your own counsel, and believing in your own infallibility. "Mitch McConnell and I spoke quite a bit in these early hours," Ryan told The New York Times later. "With McConnell's permission, I put out this massive Gantt chart." "Every time he [Trump] sent a crazy tweet or tried to derail Congress' agenda, I'd always say, 'No, remember, we have this Gantt chart, and this is what we're supposed to be doing now.'"

The chart uses horizontal bars to represent each of various projects—traditional tax cuts, deregulation, and so on—and vertical lines to represent the dates for the procedures required to complete each one. It was a handy tool, but it was completely Egghead. Ryan used the formal name of the thing as he talked about it. Many Americans, including members of Congress, are irritated by eggheads. They appear to be holier-than-thou types. (Bill Clinton is Exhibit A.) But just because Ryan veered into super-nerd territory when explaining the methodology didn't mean he and McConnell hadn't done vital work. They also used political magic to mask their true intentions by utilising phoney praise and support. Because the president's primary currency is ass-kissing—he likes to smooch and be smooched—this move provided them with the finest opportunity to have some influence. Meanwhile, Trump would continue to indulge his inclinations by employing his tried-and-true tactics of threats, punishment, and charm. As many people have said after meeting him in New York or Washington, Trump can be extremely pleasant, even enjoyable to be around. He enjoyed giving guests tours of the White House and showing them the button he used to summon a Diet Coke anytime he desired one. Trump's childish behaviour was also demonstrated in front of more significant people. The White House kitchen was put on notice that the president should always be served twice as much ice cream as anyone he invited for a private dinner, and to watch him interact with champion athletes when they visited—he offered the Clemson University football team a buffet of fast food—you'd think he was an eight-year-old at heart. His ex-wife Marla Maples described him as charming in this regard. Trump perplexed, deluded, self-indulgent, and brutal me. I expected the cold shoulder at one of our meetings because I had rejected his presidential run. Instead, he sought to win me over in what I later realised was one of his signature moves. He told the other people in the room that I looked great and performed well on TV. I knew Trump had seen me because he was addicted to cable news, frequently flicking from channel to channel, and I knew he valued performance above all else. Remember, he rose to national prominence as the mogul/host of The Apprentice, where his tagline was "You're fired!" But his reaction to me was perplexing at the time. A number of us tried to address the Chinese business ZTE, which was selling US communications gear to Iran and North Korea, during another visit to the White House. The corporation had sent microprocessors, routers, servers, and software to assist both countries in the construction of full networks. The original agreement that allowed China to receive US technology, which Silicon Valley corporations had worked hard to accomplish, had been highly contentious. According to federal specialists, the technology may be rigged to collect data that could be passed back to the seller. Given the Chinese government's stake in ZTE, the data might be utilised for a variety of malicious purposes, ranging from industrial espionage to government data gathering. We learned that ZTE executives kept the sale to North Korea and Iran hidden even from their auditors during the course of a US probe that began before Trump became president. This points to the Chinese government being engaged. Iran and North Korea were among the most dangerous countries on the earth, with their repeated pronouncements of hostile intentions toward America's friends, nuclear weapons programs, and terrorism. The entire world was counting on us to keep them at bay. Our sanctions were accompanied by a warning that countries who violated them would be barred from all future trade with the United States. The sanctions were effective because Iran and North Korea were obliged to go without key supplies and goods or pay black market prices for them. President Trump campaigned on a vow to be strong on China, which manipulated currencies and unfairly subsidised exporters, but he said he wouldn't go after ZTE because he told China's president, Xi Jinping, that he would. In fact, Trump decided to lift the penalties against ZTE after Xi complained about job losses, which he somehow related to a century of Western warfare against his country. This issue was a textbook example of the complexities of our international relations. Trump's ambition to manage through personal relationships complicates matters even further. Years later, then-national security adviser John Bolton would write about it, claiming that Trump "said he had told [Commerce Secretary Wilbur] Ross to work something out for China, to which Xi replied that if that were done, he would owe Trump a favour, and Trump immediately responded that he was doing this because of Xi.""Diplomacy is not the way to protect America's interests." But it satisfied Trump's need for self-indulgence. This instinct was on full display when I went to the White House to talk with Trump about continuing to aid and protect Syrian, Iraqi, and Turkish Kurds who were occupying refugee camps on the Turkish border; Kurdish fighters had been our fierce allies in northern Iraq and remained a great source of intelligence. Unfortunately, they were also involved in a long-running battle for political control of ethnic enclaves in Iraq, Syria, and eastern Turkey. I certainly opposed any attempt to expand this battle to Syria and believed that the Kurds deserved our assistance, if not for humanitarian reasons, then because we owed them. However, Turkey's prime minister, Recep Erdogan, who had transitioned from a democrat to a dictator, called Trump on a Sunday to urge that US troops stationed in Syria to safeguard Kurdish camps be ordered out. Trump, a self-proclaimed admirer of strongmen who counts Xi, Erdogan, and others among his pals, agreed to the request. To my dismay, as soon as our soldiers left, the Turks attacked the Kurds in Syria. Estimates of the number of Kurds slain ranged from 500 to 1500, with a further 1500 wounded. This included numerous individuals who were murdered or injured while fleeing. Trump's brutality resulted in their blood being spilled. You'd think that an encounter with Trump over the Kurds would have prepared me to vote to impeach him for his betrayal of Ukraine. When he granted Erdogan's request, the Ukraine situation was already as hot as hell. And while the Democrats investigated the incident and held hearings, I was tempted to vote to impeach him, which would be the equivalent of an indictment followed by a Senate trial. Any other president's impeachment story would be seared into your mind. Only two presidents have been impeached in the 242 years since America declared independence. In 1868, Andrew Johnson was impeached but not convicted. Clinton experienced the same scenario in 1999. Both benefited from the constitutional necessity of a two-thirds vote for conviction, and it was this high threshold, set against Trump's Senate backing, that made me nervous. If I had voted to impeach him, I would have welcomed a primary rival who would very certainly win the nomination and end my House tenure. Like everyone else in Congress, I thought my presence was important. "Indispensable" was a strong term to describe this belief. It was more like not necessary. This was an attitude I worked hard to cultivate, and if I ever lost it, my family was quick to call me on it. Many of my coworkers, based on my contacts with them, elected not to undertake this type of reality check. Spend a few days with them, and you'll observe the same thing. When I say the impeachment vote gave me pause, I don't mean that I thought Trump had done nothing wrong. He had withheld essential military aid offered by the US to

Ukraine for its fight against Russian invaders on the condition that the country's newly elected president, Volodymyr Zelenskyy, assist him in dealing with the Russia election interference scandal. Trump desired that Kyiv be shown to have interfered rather than Moscow. He also instructed Zelenskyy to look into former Vice President Joe Biden's son to assist prove that he used his father's position to receive payments from a Ukrainian energy company. Biden was already the Democratic Party's front-runner for the 2020 presidential candidacy at the time. Zelenskyy, a former actor and comedian, had performed the humorous role of a man who stumbled into the highest office in his country. When he was elected, it was mostly because voters perceived his election as a protest against pervasive corruption. In the call, Zelenskyy was outmatched, with Trump saying, "I would like you to do us a favour" in exchange for the support. According to a transcript of the call, Trump sounds like a gangster, and Zelenskyy sounds like a forlorn leader desperate to prevent the Russians, who have already captured the Crimean Peninsula and a portion of the Donbas region, from moving farther. (This is why he required the promised American equipment.) Instead, Zelenskyy was told to go after Joe Biden, whom Trump anticipated would be his 2020 opponent, and produce evidence that Biden had used his position as Obama's vice president to swindle Ukrainian businesses. Zelenskyy did not say "no" directly, but he refused to do what the American president requested. A crew of clownish characters with no government positions aided Trump's strategy. Ukrainian businessmen Lev Parnas and Igor Fruman have bought their way into Trump's orbit with large campaign contributions. They teamed up with Rudy Giuliani, who, after garnering international praise for his response to the 9/11 attacks as New York City mayor, squandered the goodwill with constant attention-seeking and the pursuit of big salaries for political consultancy. He had previously pursued Trump's nomination for Secretary of State. The closest he'd go was introducing himself as "President Trump's attorney" in order to obtain access to European officials and undercut the real diplomats. The Ukraine affair was exposed by a whistleblower who was supported by other witnesses but was demonised at every move by Trump's congressional supporters. The Democrat-controlled House began its investigation with hearings in a secure, below-ground spy-proof room known as the sensitive compartmented information facility (SCIF). The SCIF was generally confined to committee members, but due to the nature of the proceedings, it was open to outsiders. The size of the room, however, limited their number. Some of my more radical coworkers would storm the SCIF and breach its security. A few moderates joined in, which disappointed me. Some of them told me it was a simple way to show support for Trump without facing major consequences.

As the impeachment vote approached, I chastised Trump for instilling fear and wrath (a tendency of his) by claiming the push represented "treason." He retweeted fundamentalist preacher Robert Jeffress's warning that it will result in "a civil war-like fracture." Jeffress was one of a number of Christian leaders that praised Trump's heinous behaviour. Franklin Graham, a nationally known preacher, for example, abandoned his father Bill's legendary and effective neutrality to become a shameless Trump booster. He compared Republicans who opposed Trump to "Judas," making the profane and immoral president Jesus Christ. When the treason and civil war remarks were made, I felt compelled to respond, stressing that since presidents are expected to keep the country united, these sentiments were "beyond repugnant."

Trump's actions, the testimony of dozens of witnesses who testified before House committees, and documentary proof all added up to a convincing case for impeachment, but supporting it would necessitate an act of rebellion that I wasn't willing to commit. As they rushed to finish their report and request a vote before the 2019 Christmas break, the Democrats handed themselves and others an out. They rationalised their decision by claiming that January 1 will mark the start of 2020 and another presidential campaign, and they didn't want to complicate matters by waiting. Republicans, on the other hand, could argue that every year is a campaign year, and that moving so swiftly reflected a lack of seriousness.

I never defended Trump against the allegations and left open the prospect of voting to impeach him. But, with every other Republican voting no, I couldn't see being the caucus' lone vote for the Democrats. I was aware that Liz Cheney of Wyoming, the second Republican who really considered voting yes, had ultimately opted to vote against the articles of impeachment. The timing and deficiencies in the Judiciary Committee's case presented to the House made it simpler for me to march with my side. Furthermore, the House managers who would prosecute the case were unlikely to receive two-thirds of the votes. The outcome in the Senate was exactly what I expected, with one slight exception. Utah Republican Mitt Romney voted to convict Trump on the allegation of abuse of authority. In the process, he became the first senator to vote to convict his own party's deposed president. In this scenario, he was a bigger outlaw than I was. Do I wish I had taken a similar stance and accepted the consequences? I do when I consider what happened after that. If I hadn't caved in to the pressure from my colleagues, I could have provided cover for others who were on the fence. In turn, we could have shown the country that the system is not as broken as they believe. Instead, I went along with it, believing Trump would be humbled. He didn't. In reality, things would deteriorate significantly. So, yeah, I'm sorry. I regret it "a lot," as he may say.

CHAPTER 9
DO YOUR JOB

On January 9, they completed the installation of the black steel perimeter fence that encircles the Capitol. It was seven feet tall and, by design, impossible to scale. It raised and dipped with the slope of the famed hill, completely separating the people from the People's House as a metaphor of our democracy's condition of crisis. Every time it drew my attention, my heart fell. Then, just as the committee convened to investigate the attack, labourers began dismantling it. You had to wonder if the barriers between the people and the facts about January 6th would be lifted as well.

We had to engage a large staff to investigate, conduct interviews, and evaluate hundreds of thousands of pages of text, including documents, letters, and memos. This required over 100 lawyers, investigators, supervisors, and support personnel. With the labour done by members and aides from our legislative offices, a total of 120 persons were involved. Even with all of this labour and some basic document-processing equipment, the staff struggled to keep up with the influx of interviews and documents. We would eventually accumulate over a thousand interviews, a million papers, and hundreds of hours of staff-reviewed film. The recordings depict events from over a hundred different perspectives given by security cameras, cell phones, social media posts, and film captured by news crews and documentarians.

Denver Riggleman, a former Republican member of Congress who was beaten in a primary by a Trumpist and had previously worked in data management, volunteered to assist with data management. He'd be working on the hundreds of thousands of text and phone records we'd gotten from witnesses and carriers. These were not recordings of real conversations or messages, but simply logs of which numbers were linked and when. It was technically possible to associate the phone numbers with specific people, map out the times they spoke, and compare them to critical events—prosecutors do this all the time, albeit with significantly fewer data points. This information would allow us to not only determine who contacted whom, but also to ask intelligent questions of those who created these connections. Rather than asking, "Did you, Mr. Z, ever reach out to Mr. Y?" we could say, "We know you called Mr. Y five times on this date." Why?"

Riggleman came up with a solution to streamline the process after a few months of study, but implementing the software would be costly. It's like a million dollars. The choice on whether to pursue this proposal became delayed. Then, with phone providers likely to begin wiping records older than a year, a common procedure for some, the entire proposal was abandoned. To say Riggleman was let down would be an understatement.

The million-dollar choice was almost certainly made in Speaker Pelosi's office. In fact, despite her commitment to stay out of the way, it became evident early on that she couldn't help but intervene. The Democrats on the committee seemed to accept this, as if the Speaker had been practising this type of leadership since she became the top leader of the congressional Democrats in 2003, which meant her caucus had nearly two decades of experience with her strong hand.

Of course, the Speaker does not state she will use her authority anytime she feels like it. In fact, when our committee first met, she summoned us to her office and told us, "I believe in you guys." I'm not going to participate. I'll leave you to your business." She then delegated one of her assistants, Jamie Fleet, to act as her eyes and ears within our offices. Fleet was a wise man who recognized and even sympathised with our difficulties. However, when I requested him to assist me with another matter, he refused. And, with the Democrats always folding their cards, Pelosi got her way whenever she wanted, which was happily not often. Democrats on the committee included Mississippi Chairman Bennie Thompson, Florida's Stephanie Murphy, Maryland's Jamie Raskin, and Virginia's Elaine Luria. They were joined by three members of Pelosi's California Mafia: Zoe Lofgren from the Bay Area, Adam Schiff from Los Angeles, and Pete Aguilar from Riverside. I was one of the group's two Republicans. Liz Cheney was the other. Despite the fact that the committee included five high-powered lawyers, the members came from a variety of backgrounds. Luria had served in the Navy. Murphy has previously worked in the Pentagon as well as as a business school lecturer. Aguilar formerly worked in the administration of California Governor Gray Davis and was the mayor of Redlands, California. Thompson had previously worked as a teacher. I grew to admire everyone on the committee. Adam Schiff and I had a previous friendship that grew considerably stronger. As a Republican, I was instructed to despise him because he was such an effective and persistent questioner at high-profile hearings. Being on the same team for the first time made me realise his knowledge, generosity to other team members, and sense of humour. I believe our bond was cemented when I referred to myself as Adam Junior and him as Adam Senior. (After all, he is my senior.) We became easygoing friends from then on. Bennie was such a serene leader that it appeared he wasn't leading at all. What I've realised is that he was a Zen master of collegiality. He was courteous, attentive, and never dismissed anyone. He appeared to understand, however, that things had a way of sorting themselves out. But if he had a shortcoming, it was that he was too kind to reporters, who have a way of cornering members whether or not they want to talk. They wait outside the chamber door and in the corridors outside members' offices, or they simply cruise the tunnels that connect the office buildings to the Capitol. Most are decent enough, even if they are always seeking a controversial statement. For some reason, Bennie couldn't be moved by these individuals, so anytime microphones were pushed in front of him, he respectfully responded. This generated some problems since every time he was asked the major question—when is the committee holding public hearings?—he sought to give an optimistic answer. This meant that from the fall of 2021 to the commencement of hearings in June 2022, the start date appeared to be pushed back every few months, however this was not the reality. We divided the committee staff into five groups, with each group in charge of performing the great majority of interviews and collecting all of the documentation. However, it was decided that committee members would take part in high-level witness interviews, including some that took place in public sessions. These included the president's closest aides as well as those active in lobbying for the gathering of enraged Trumpists and directing events on the ground as the attack began and advanced. We also decided on the paperwork we intended to give to the American people so that no one could question who, what, how, or why things happened the way they did. For lack of a better phrase, our model became the must-watch limited series seen on streaming

TV services. Our "series" would last eight "episodes" and be supported by a lengthy written report with thousands of endnotes, similar to those published by investigative committees. As the "hosts" of the series, we were each allocated episodes to chair. I was picked to lead the fifth hearing because it would focus on how many public officials violated their oaths, and how others who should have known better engaged in a coup attempt unbefitting patriots. I was picked because I am not an attorney, and we anticipated that people would understand the legal principles if they were conveyed by someone who was not a lawyer.

My second duty, which I shared with Elaine Luria, was to conduct a hearing on the day of the attempted coup and, more importantly, the 187-minute period between Trump being aware of the attack on the Capitol and his call for its termination. Elaine and I were appointed in this case, I believe, because we were both military personnel who had taken and kept oaths of office and understood how to operate in a crisis. In contrast, the president lacked crisis management skills and had violated his oath of office. We weren't lawyers, and what was necessary was a straightforward telling of a story that didn't require any lawyerly touches. This was especially true in light of Trump's failure to intervene to stop the bloodshed. He knew what was going on because he had positioned himself in front of television news. McCarthy was even phoned to implore him to act, but he refused. As much as the public hungered for the gripping story we needed to convey, we on the committee were resolved to accomplish the work in an orderly way. As anyone who watched the hearings could see, Liz was the most forceful and fully informed member of the committee. She left no doubt that she saw Trump as a grave danger, and that the January 6 attack was the result of his lies, inflammatory rhetoric, and irresponsibility. (If I were qualified to diagnose Trump with a mental condition, I'd offer it here. Instead, I can just say, in colloquial terms: the guy is nucking futs.)

Within the group, Liz often refocused us when we veered away from the fundamental problem of the coup, but she could do this in a sandpapery way that left some individuals feeling hurt. Actually, she probably rubbed every one of us the wrong way at one time or another. This was due to her intensity and candour—as well as her superior knowledge. In these ways, she reminded me of her father, the former vice president. He wasn't particularly endearing, but he was extremely effective. Like father, like daughter.

At the start of 2022, when we seemed a bit stalled, the chairman scheduled a one-day retreat at the Library of Congress to deal with conflict in the group. The world's largest library, it occupies four enormous buildings, but the most famous one is the imposing, late-nineteenth-century structure that occupies an entire city block facing the East Front of the Capitol. It took eleven years to build. The exterior is heavily ornamented with elements taken from the Paris Opera House. Visitors climb past the famed statues of Neptune's Court to enter on the second floor. The inside of the library is dominated by an enormous circular main reading room. An overhead shot in the film All the President's Men reveals the grandeur of this room with a rising perspective until you see more than a hundred desks arranged in the big circles split by eight aisles that look like sun rays from a height. At one point during the conference, Liz recommended we enter the reading room reserved for members of Congress. We couldn't help but be moved by the original handwritten copy of the Gettysburg Address, one of only five in existence, which had been brought into the room at Liz's request. I won't say we faced a challenge remotely comparable to Lincoln's, but we were dealing with an event unprecedented in our history—a coup attempt fueled by a president—and the American people, including future generations, would judge our response. Here I would like to quote a blog post by Library of Congress staffer Donna Sokol, who describes a mosaic titled The Law, which dominates the room. At the centre a woman representing Law sits on a throne. Sokol writes: The right side of the mosaic portrays three figures—Fraud, Discord, and Violence—that represent the result of a lawless land. Fraud uses her robe to conceal the facts about her illegal actions. Discord is home to two duelling snakes, whose confused entanglement will lead to each snake's demise from his own venom. Violence is clad in a helmet, clutches a sword, and keeps a burning torch nearby. We observe two discarded things on this trio's side of the throne—a law book and the scales of justice, signifying their contempt for the law.

The left side of the mosaic shows what happens when the rule of law functions well: Industry, Peace, and Truth. Industry is a young man with a hammer and a wheel alongside him. Peace holds an olive branch and wears an olive branch crown as a symbol of peace. Truth, unlike her foil, Fraud, is unashamedly uncovered and holds lilies, which in this context symbolises innocence. On their side of the throne, two doves represent peace—the result of a lawful existence.

The mosaic accurately depicted our committee's position. On one side we confronted the evils of fraud (Trump's lies), discord (created by his enablers), and violence as it was perpetrated by his followers on January 6. We'd reached the point where we needed to focus harder. Liz, who had identified Trump as the most dangerous leader in our history, wanted us to include him in every chapter of the story. No one would argue with this point, but some wanted to focus on related issues. For example, Jamie Raskin suggested that we focus on how the Electoral College system enabled Trump's deception. The college had been designed to balance the influence of states with bigger and smaller populations. Though necessary for national unity at the moment, this strategy clearly contradicted democracy's one-man, one-vote foundation. The founders also set circumstances for the confusion Trump fostered by requiring a drawn-out process for gathering and validating results. This made sense in the era of Paul Revere's ride, and it worked—until someone devoted solely to his own power used the weeks between the election and certification to convince half of the country that evil was at work, and tens of thousands became so agitated that they felt compelled to act. This is as good a place as any to mention Trump's creation of an alternate reality inhabited by his followers, who were poised to become action-figure heroes. First, Trump had been spreading scepticism about the election system for at least five years. After losing in 2020, he told the Big Lie about how the worst had happened. His prophecy had come true. His most ardent supporters, primed to believe, filled with patriotic dreams, and continually outraged with the government, felt the time had come to act. But, like Fundamentalists who unite behind a preacher who reads Scripture they don't comprehend, Trump's marauders were ignorant of current events, American history, and the Constitution while oozing with phoney righteousness. They donned their costumes—combat gear, Revolutionary War garb, Trump memorabilia, and even cartoon character costumes—and transformed into a snarling, angry mob. I wanted to join Jamie in emphasising how the Electoral College paved the way for disaster. I agreed with him that the Electoral College should be eliminated, but I didn't want to go that far. Pursuing this reform to address a background element will divert attention away from our efforts to convey the truth about January 6. Stephanie Murphy's intention to focus on the security flaws uncovered by the attack was similar, albeit to a lesser extent. The Capitol Police had failed to recognize the threat and had not deployed a sufficient force. Those on duty lacked the necessary equipment, and their communications and coordination fell apart almost immediately. However, when all of the circumstances in the police response are considered, it becomes more difficult to criticise. Unlike the District of Columbia police, who deal with protests and the danger of civil disorder virtually every day, Capitol Police had never seen anything remotely resembling what happened on January 1, 2021. A hundred officers stood on their side, barely armed and increasingly worried. On the other side raged a mob large enough to fill the local NBA arena and better equipped than the cops. Capitol Police were certain that many people in the crowd had sidearms and were concerned that drawing their own firearms or firing a warning shot would start an uncontrollable gun battle. With no plan for arresting and holding criminals, the Capitol Police performed valiantly, delaying the mob until everyone inside could flee or find safe cover. However, Liz was concerned that focusing on the cops would quickly develop into a victim-blaming scenario. Over a hundred officers had been injured. As a result of his injuries, one had perished. Two of them had committed suicide only a few days following their horrific encounters. The cops had already implemented modifications and were working on more. Besides, as a Cheney official later said, "the Capitol didn't attack itself."

The library room's intimate and stimulating atmosphere made it reasonably easy to reach an agreement. We decided that while the Electoral College challenges and worries about Capitol protection would be highlighted, neither would be the focus of rigorous study or recommendations. We also started addressing an essential question: Would the report include a series of clear suggestions, or would it simply analyse and draw conclusions about what happened before, during, and after the riots?

Despite the fact that scores of witnesses violated subpoenas and refused to come before the committee, the witnesses who did appear might be grouped into three groups. The first group, which I would describe as Trump-infected zombies, declined to answer questions, invoking their Fifth Amendment privilege against self-incrimination. Like parasitic worms, the man's words had taken over their minds, rendering them pathologically faithful and incapable of autonomous thought.

Roger Stone was the best example of a Trump zombie, having taken the Fifth Amendment more than seventy times. Stone is a particularly unpleasant figure who has captivated the political press for more than fifty years. Part of his act involves his wearing bizarre outfits: if you check online, you'll find him dressed like Mr. Peanut. He dressed down for us, but he still had an ultra-wide-collared shirt and a silver silk hankie tucked casually into the pocket of his suit jacket. He is a man who frequently comes with thuggish young bodyguards, and his frightened refusals to connect with us were amusing.

Another zombie was John Eastman, a legal professor who warned Trump that Vice President Mike Pence would interfere with Electoral College qualifications. He referred to the Fifth 150 times. Eastman's evasion came to be portrayed as more pitiful than hilarious, given his national reputation for making unconventional legal claims. Everyone knew, of course, that he had reversed himself on the Pence issue, first telling Trump that there was nothing the vice president could do and then arguing that Pence could simply set aside enough state filings to call Biden's election into question as he presided over the largely ceremonial certification process. If he had spoken, the only explanation he could have given would have put him in an intellectual bind, forcing him to defend what was an evident manoeuvre in Trump's favour. I couldn't help but wonder if Eastman expected to be nominated attorney general if the coup succeeded and the president managed to stay in office.

The second group of witnesses I would describe as "partial zombies." Although the Make America Great Again worms were present, there were areas of their brains that were less affected and allowed for some individual thought or courage. Rudy Giuliani, a partly zombie, evaded inquiries about his role in propagating the Big Lie. His memory failed him at numerous convenient (for him) times. He also made several irrelevant remarks, including an assault on Hillary Clinton, and gave unsubstantiated conclusions about "massive [election] cheating" in areas like Philadelphia. Giuliani further stated that during the numerous phone conversations he made to Trump on the evening of January 6, he urged him to continue battling to prevent the certification. Overall, his evidence contained so much deflection and deception that it validated the public's perception that the once great leader who united New York in the aftermath of 9/11 had devolved into a blithering servant of a guy who never earned his attention.

The third and last group of witnesses consisted of men and women of character who had been part of Trump's team, either inside the administration or in his political operation, and who had shown some courage as the January 6 attack approached and subsequently occurred. They had advised higher-ups, and in some cases the president himself, not to inflame his followers, and they had asked their superiors to do something to stop the riot at the Capitol during and after the rally.

Truth-teller Cassidy Hutchinson, an aide to White House Chief of Staff Mark Meadows, informed us that White House officials were aware that the violence-prone Proud Boys and Oath Keepers would be present at the Ellipse rally. She claimed that on the day of the rally, Trump complained that attendees were taking too long to pass through weapon-screening magnetometers and that he wanted the safety screening to be lifted because he believed they were not there to harm HIM. One of the more heinous incidents she told, a secondhand account later confirmed, was Trump's demand that he be transported to the Capitol following the rally. When security personnel declined, citing the risk, Trump rushed into the rear of the car, grabbed the driver, and demanded again. It was ineffective. Sarah Matthews, Trump's former deputy press secretary, testified that in the early stages of the attack, Mark Meadows heard desperate pleas from aides and outside advisers that Trump call off the horde but remained in his office because the president "wanted to be alone." Meadows was glancing at his phone screen when White House counsel Pat Cipollone stormed into his office, demanding that something be done to put an end to the ruckus. When Matthews stopped by Meadows' office a few minutes later, she noticed that he was still engrossed in his phone.

Meadows' statement matched the man I knew in the House, when he represented a North Carolina district from 2013 until 2020. Meadows had been the Freedom Caucus leader and one of Kevin McCarthy's most important allies. He was also the type of politician who would slap you on the back in one minute and then stab you in the next. weirdly, or perhaps not so weirdly, he had sold land in Colorado to a nutty creationist group who denied earth science and the theory of evolution and erroneously claimed that a band of homeschoolers had unearthed a dinosaur there. As their film about the finding slid into the obscurity reserved for radicals, Meadows stood by its makers. Meadows was an intelligent guy. He had to know the assertions in the film were hokum. But the stand united him with politically strong Fundamentalists, and that was what mattered to him. Due to the social distance measures put in place to deal with the epidemic and so that we could observe the proceedings from our district, most members of the committee viewed the deposition via video conference links. Despite the persecution I received in public settings, I still liked my city and district.

When we began relaying the tale of January 6 in public hearings that drew millions of TV viewers, video would take the role of in-person work. Chairman Thompson and Vice Chairperson Cheney delivered opening speeches at each hearing. While Thompson calmly predicted the horrific testimony that would follow in each case, it was Cheney's statements that were the most piercing.

Cheney talks with her father's candour and a degree of scathing insight so tinged with common sense that no one could possibly miss her point. "President Trump is a seventy-six-year-old man," she said during one hearing. "He is not an impressionable child." During the same session, she stated that "Donald Trump cannot escape responsibility by being willfully blind."

Although she was stern in her views about the probe, Cheney demonstrated a sensitive side when dealing with the truthful and hence risk-taking witnesses, particularly after sessions were adjourned. Cassidy Hutchinson is depicted shutting her eyes and smiling as Cheney offers her a hug in one classic shot from the day of her testimony.

Although you would believe that experienced members of Congress question witnesses in reaction to their statements or respond spontaneously when given the opportunity to speak, this is not the case when committees conduct complex investigations. I was grateful for the formal preparation we went through as I prepared to chair the fifth hearing, which would focus on the Justice Department and January 6. It was similar to what I would expect casts to do before a live TV broadcast, such as Saturday Night Live, with read-throughs and modifications done around a table and then rehearsals in the Cannon House Office Building Caucus Room, which is Capitol Hill's largest meeting area.

With millions of people watching the broadcast proceedings, the probe quickly assumed cultural significance. SNL's "cold open" in October 2022 focused on the committee, which was described as a group of "monotone nerds." To my surprise, I made it into the sketch, where the actor impersonating me begged for one of the cupcakes given by "Bennie Thompson" to thank us at the end of the hearing. "I" reappeared to reveal that I had taken a cupcake and then displayed all of the witnesses who had alerted Trump that he had lost the election, including a German dog. "I" also had the opportunity to mispronounce my own name and join the ensemble in exclaiming, "Live from New York, it's Saturday Night." It appeared that the committee had become culturally significant.

I was concerned as the hearing approached, but I was relieved to know that I had gone over the material numerous times. We had practised, and most importantly, my coworkers had my back. "I remember making a commitment, out loud a few times and in my heart repeatedly even today, that if we are going to ask Americans to die in service to our country, we as leaders must at least be willing to sacrifice our political careers when integrity and our oath require it," I said before beginning to present evidence. After all, losing a job is little in comparison to losing your life."

During the hearing, we on the committee demonstrated how top Justice Department officials had rejected pressure to follow Trump's demands. (He requested that they proclaim the election "corrupt" and then "leave the rest to me and the Republican Congressmen.") The committee staff aired supporting footage from depositions of several witnesses who backed up what I said when I presented the evidence. The video made the presentation easier to follow and saved people from sitting through the type of drawn-out questioning that occurs during live testimony, where, let's face it, members often compete for time in order to raise their profile in the media and demonstrate their importance to those back home.

Some of the most damaging films included a lower-level Justice Department official named Jeffrey Clark, who pledged to conduct investigations that he was certain would uncover massive fraud. However, he could only do so under a new attorney general. Who could that be? Jeffrey Clark suggested Jeffrey Clark. Surprisingly, Clark did not obtain the job.

Anyone who doubted the Trump team's involvement in the January 6 attacks just had to look at the video we showed of a MAGA man standing outside the Department of Justice building on his route from the Ellipse to the Capitol. "Do your job! Do your job!" Do your job! "Do your job! Do your job!" he yelled. "We're marching to the Capitol from here in DC." We're at the Department of Justice right now, telling these powers to do their jobs!"

Rep. Louie Gohmert repeated "do your job" in a montage of extreme-right members of Congress—Paul Gosar, Jim Jordan, Mo Brooks, Matt Gaetz, and others—who warned, among other things, that on January 6, patriots would begin "taking down names and kicking ass." Although I had seen all of this film previously, seeing it displayed in a packed hearing room and knowing it was being broadcast across America and the world gave me shivers. As the fast-paced session concluded, I believed we had demonstrated, in a convincing manner, the several ways in which Trump attempted to corrupt the Justice Department in order to use its work as a cover for destroying democracy. He had pressed Attorney General Bill Barr to launch a major investigation into voter fraud (Barr declined), and he had stressed that if his successor did it, he could simply "say it [the election] was corrupt and leave the rest to me and the Republican congressmen." Barr's replacement, Jeffrey Rosen, likewise refused. Trump then attempted to place a flunky in Rosen's position, but was foiled only when he discovered that key justice officials would quit if he did. Trump had used legal actions such as litigation to lend legitimacy to his assertions throughout his life. This had worked, at least in terms of catching the attention of reporters who, eager for a story, would gladly assist the hoax. This time, however, Trump encountered people of integrity who indicated that many authorities recognize they owe devotion not to one person, even if he is the president, but to the position they hold and the nation. People he sought to push around did their jobs despite the fact that the stakes were significantly higher than a simple publicity war.

CHAPTER 10
THE FINAL HEARING

My personal experience on January 6 was never far from my mind as I prepared to address the eighth and last planned hearing with my colleague Elaine Luria. We were required to summarise the material presented in earlier sessions, similar to the last episode of a TV show, and draw major conclusions. We prefaced the discussion with the phrase "Dereliction of Duty."

I was positive that this title was appropriate, just as I was certain that by agreeing to join the committee as a Republican, I was doing the right thing. But it was not a simple task. Indeed, as I travelled back and forth to my district, I experienced the kind of shunning that religious sects impose on disobedient members, as well as threatening letters, which were made all the more upsetting because they were sent to our home and sometimes addressed to Sofia.

One particularly horrible letter, written by a professing believer, was addressed to my wife. He or she wrote in it, "Although it may take some time, he [I] will be executed." But don't worry, you and Christian will join Adam in Hell as well! We think it's blasphemous that you named the Devil's son Christian!" I could tell he or she was mimicking Trump's style because of the excessive punctuation and weirdly positioned capital letters. So was the hypocrisy evident in a pledge of murder made by someone claiming the wrath of "God Fearing Christians."

The abrupt moves against me by a party I had served for twenty years were less repulsive, but just as insane. Dozens of county chairpersons spoke out against my impeachment vote. Two Trump fans have indicated that they will run against me in the next Republican primary, and protesters have held rallies in which they have stated that they would not even support me in a fight for dogcatcher. A Republican consultant flew into the district and stated that he would train people to oppose me. Others who had defied the bully president were met with the same animosity from local party officials. It should be emphasised that several of these party officials rose to power during the Trump administration, replacing more traditional Republicans. They would have to bring him water if they wanted to preserve their places.

All of this hostility had prompted me to declare that I would not run for reelection. I became the second of ten House Republicans to support impeachment. "My passion for this country has only grown," I stated as I explained my decision. My passion to make a difference is stronger than ever. My dissatisfaction with non-leaders is profound. The fight must be considerably larger, and the facts must reach all of the American people."

Trump's response—"2 down, 8 to go!"—reiterated his pledge to ending the congressional careers of any Republican who voted to impeach him and warned everyone else that they would meet the same fate if they did not exhibit Mafia-style allegiance to the big boss. The media concentrated on whether I would run for Senate, governor, or even president, hoping to capitalise on the respect I was receiving from both moderates and leftists. To do this as a Republican, I'd have to win a primary, and I didn't stand a snowball's chance in hell of doing so. The second alternative was to run as an independent, which, like most independent candidacies, may be a waste of time. When it came to the president, I said to myself, "You can't be serious."

In the end, I opted not to run for any of the positions that were proposed to me. I was tired of Congress, so the Senate didn't seem appealing. Is it even possible for me to envisage myself in the governor's house or the White House? No. Besides, I had a young son, Christian, and a girlfriend in Sofia who were both expecting me. There was also Country First, which was rapidly growing and would aid my efforts on the side of democracy. And, of course, the January 6 committee resumed its work, allowing me to investigate the violent attack that I felt directly touched me.

When Elaine and I shared the 187-minute gap presentation, people seemed most impressed by witnesses who described Trump staying in a dining room near the Oval Office, watching TV, speaking to outside advisers (two calls with Rudy Giuliani), and receiving but ignoring reports on the violence being carried out in his name. As numerous Fox News commentators pleaded with him to act, including several from my angry cousin's pantheon, Trump hesitated, preferring to just watch his troops fight, much like a mounted eighteenth-century general watching a war from a hilltop. Of course, presidents are not meant to sit on their hands as a calamity unfolds. This is why the evening's subject was "Dereliction of Duty."

During my speech, I said, "He [President Trump] told Mark Meadows that the rioters were doing what they should be doing, and the rioters understood they were doing what President Trump wanted them to do." Meanwhile, the president's daughter Ivanka and son Donald Jr. pleaded with him to stop the mob. Trump did not do anything. He intentionally refused to respond to a summons from the Pentagon, which was in the midst of mobilising the National Guard.

One of the most satisfying pieces of evidence we were able to provide showed Senator Josh Hawley pumping an encouraging fist toward the mob gathered for the attack outside the Capitol. Hawley had stated his intention to vote against certifying results in many states. This gesture enraged the audience and was again rebroadcast in numerous media sites. We showed a video of Hawley literally running from the throng, which was ignored. A before-and-after exhibit had rarely represented both a guy's desire to fight and the man in flight.

One of the most incriminating pieces of evidence was Trump editing a statement he delivered the day after the riot, when the country was reeling from what it had experienced and much of the world was stunned by the spectacle of a great democracy brought low. It shows that he had crossed out the comment about being "sickened" by the violence, as well as the phrase "you do not represent me." You will not be "prosecuted to the fullest extent of the law." He also lied about how he used the National Guard (he did not). In an audio recording, he states, "I don't want to say the election is over, I just want to say Congress has certified the results without saying the election is over, okay?" That's exactly what he did.

In my last statement, I summarised what I had learned and what I feared:

Whatever your politics are, or how you feel about the election results, we as Americans must all agree on this. Donald Trump's actions on January 6th were a flagrant violation of his oath of office and a terrible abdication of duty to our country.

It's a blot on our past. It is a disgrace to all those who have given their lives and sacrificed for our democracy. When we provide our entire findings, we will recommend legislative and policy measures to prevent another January sixth. The reason this is critical is that the forces Donald Trump sparked that day have not subsided.

Militant, intolerant ideologies, militias, alienation and disaffection, strange fancies and disinformation are all still ready to go. That is the obnoxious elephant in the room. But if January 6th reminded us of anything, I hope it was this: laws are simply words on paper.

They are meaningless in the absence of public workers committed to the rule of law and held accountable by a public that believes oaths matter—oaths that matter more than party tribalism or the cheap thrill of earning political points. We, the people, must demand more from our elected officials and ourselves. Oaths are important.

The contents of this book may not be copied, reproduced or transmitted without the express written permission of the author or publisher. Under no circumstances will the publisher or author be responsible or liable for any damages, compensation or monetary loss arising from the information contained in this book, whether directly or indirectly. .

Disclaimer Notice:

Although the author and publisher have made every effort to ensure the accuracy and completeness of the content, they do not, however, make any representations or warranties as to the accuracy, completeness, or reliability of the content. , suitability or availability of the information, products, services or related graphics contained in the book for any purpose. Readers are solely responsible for their use of the information contained in this book

Every effort has been made to make this book possible. If any omission or error has occurred unintentionally, the author and publisher will be happy to acknowledge it in upcoming versions.